Kate Russell

Off the Sick List!

How to Turn Employee Absence Into Attendance

Foreword by Bob Champion MBE

Paperback ISBN 978-0-9546054-4-5

Published in the UK by MX Publishing

335 Princess Park Manor, Royal Drive, London, N11 3GX.

Cover design by C Designs

Other books by the same author: 101 Tips for Employers - The Briefcase Bible To Employment Questions

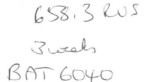

Praise for Off The Sick List!

A very useful reference guide, with simple and effective tools and processes to handle the awkward area of employee absence. In particular, how to question the short term absence was great - the questions to pose were excellent. *Sharon Emecz, Head of Marketing, GW Professional*

Once again Kate has provided just what we need; a step by step guide through the minefield of dealing with staff absence. Terrified of being blown away by the intricacies of employment law? Step carefully in Kate's clearly marked footprints and you will be safe! As always she has written in plain English, reinforcing her guidance with helpful real cases. A must have on the desk of today's manager. *John Langridge, Manager, Green Pastures*

Off the Sick List! is one of the most practical, easy to digest and factual books I have read about this current and problematic business area, whilst still being comprehensive and covering all the various issues which every manager faces in their day-to-day working lives. The case studies in this book are extremely helpful and makes the whole area of employee absence not only so much easier to understand but also very intuitive. This book is a must for all managers and reduces the need for seeking the guidance from legal firms or HR departments! *Trudy Sefton, Director, Impact Learning Solutions*

Straight forward, easy to follow guidance, practical and jargon free. *Stuart Tinkler, HR Manager, Saffron Housing*

Comprehensive, practical and informative advice written in an easily understood style. Relevant case law examples help to demonstrate the practicalities of how to apply the right approach and also raise awareness of the many pitfalls in today's employment legislation. This book is a valuable guide for managers and HR practitioners with lots of useful references to external resources which are available for specific assistance. The guidance on managing workplace stress is particularly helpful, with excellent advice on applying the right balance of fairness to both the employer and employee. The appendices are extremely useful in terms of setting up best practice policies for managing absence. *Karen Shearing, HR Administrator, Jas Bowman & Sons Ltd*

I thoroughly enjoyed reading this book. It is extremely informative and practical but with a wry sense of humour scattered throughout. *Barbara Farren, HR Partner, Bishop Grosseteste University College*

It is unusual to find a book written by a lawyer which is full of down to earth practical advice presented in an easily digested and light-hearted format. This is just such a book.

Miss Russell has immense experience in helping employers manage the problems posed by employee's absence in all its forms, from long-term illness to Mondayitis. She wears her learning lightly and does not overpower her readers with legal jargon.

Several sections of the book made me smile, especially the sections on return to work meetings and the Headmistress technique. That said, the book has a serious purpose in assisting managers who have to deal with them do so effectively and avoid the minefields of disability discrimination and unfair dismissal.

The book contains useful sections on obtaining and using medical advice and handling stress at work. It also contains a number of useful sample letters and other materials. It should be on the bookshelf of every businessman and woman who has to deal with staff issues as part of their stock in trade. *Hywel Griffith, Employment Law Partner, Kester Cunningham John*

I found *Off the Sick List!* both a good reference guide and useful tool for developing an effective absence management procedure.

It is a good read, which covers all of the relevant points regarding managing attendance and the relevant culture associated with this. It is also easy to read (unlike others) and gives a good insight into the legal aspects. *David Law, Public Service organization South Wales*

Employee absence not only hits your bottom line profit, it has a hidden impact on staff morale, quality and your line managers' sanity! Even in the unlikely event that sickness absence is not a problem in your organization who is to say you won't have one in the near future. Use Kate's *Off the Sick List!* to develop a fair and effective procedure to save yourself time and money. You will regret it if you don't!

I have used the advice described in this book to reduce my organization's absence level to below that of the national average. This has reduced our costs, increased employee morale and made our company a better place for all to work. *Graham Wellings, Production Manager, FCC (Europe) Ltd*

The book was an easy read which provides sensible, tried and trusted advice to both HR and line managers in a pragmatic and accessible style. Good use has been made of legal cases which illustrated the need for early corrective coaching, intervention and control.

Kate's approach is that positive and proactive attitudes by management will often turn a chronic absentee into one that can contribute at higher levels and for longer – in my experience some employees don't begin to understand the link between their own attendance and overall team performance until they hear what the 'Head Mistress' has to say. *Steve Williamson, Group HR Manager, Somerston Hotels Ltd*

As a small business owner I only employ a couple of staff, and each person is crucial to my business. It is imperative that they are well motivated, performing well and above all actually present in their roles. Therefore to have a book that is well written, easy to read and understand, with practical suggestions to manage and improve absenteeism is a godsend. There are some excellent ideas in this book which are easy to remember and implement, backed up with case studies and examples that most businesses will associate with. Any manager who is responsible for improving or maintaining attendance levels should read this book. *Trevor Nicholls, Director, Best of Milton Keynes*

About the Author

Kate Russell BA (Hons), Barrister, MA

After studying for a business law degree, Kate qualified as a barrister. She moved to industry, gaining several years experience in operations, moved into human resources and later became a training specialist working in the manufacturing, distribution and service sectors.

She started Russell Personnel & Training in 1998 and now divides her time between advising small and medium sized businesses on HR issues and delivering a range of highly practical employment law awareness training to line managers, including a range of public workshops. Her unusual combination of legal background, direct line management experience and HR skills, enable Kate to present the stringent requirements of the law balanced against the realities of working life. She is a senior presenter for several companies and a popular public speaker. Kate completed a MA in strategic human resource management in 2004.

She is the author of several practical employment handbooks and e-books and the highly acclaimed audio update service, *Law on the Move*, as well as a monthly e-newsletter, the latter document neatly combining the useful, topical and the frivolous.

For more information about Russell Personnel & Training, go to www.russell-personnel.com

Acknowledgements

Thanks are due to a number of people who have helped me to produce *Off the Sick List!*

The book wouldn't have come about if it wasn't for the experiences gained over the years with my clients' employees. The experiences have ranged from the very straightforward to the extremely knotty and the cases have been fascinating, challenging and occasionally very sad. I am firmly convinced that I have the most fantastic clients one could ever wish for (cheesy but true) and I'm grateful that I've had the chance to work with them.

Caroline Massingham deserves a medal, partly for her great cover design, but mostly because I vacillate madly when it comes to things like this and I must have changed my mind at least a dozen times.

Thanks to all reviewers who read the book and provided feedback and for all the firm words (yet again!) about the finer points of my use of commas, especially from Angharad Hills and David Kinder.

Finally, thanks to my team. Katie Oakley and Leigh Brannon have worked hard to iron out the blips, keep me to the time table and provided distraction and tea when I got stuck.

In memory of Freda

who would have greatly enjoyed 'the headmistress technique'

Statutory Limits

Today's limits have not been specified in this book because they go out of date so quickly. You can email **info@russell-personnel.com** for an up-to-date copy of statutory limits.

Keeping Up To Date

Keep up to date with our free e-newsletter by emailing subscribe@russell-personnel.com

Disclaimer

Note

For convenience and brevity I have referred to 'he' and 'him' throughout the book. It is intended to refer to both male and female employees.

Abbreviations

ACAS	Advice, Conciliation and Arbitration Service
CA	Court of Appeal
CIPD	Chartered Institute of Personnel & Development
DBERR	Dept for Business Enterprise & Regulatory Reform
DDA	Disability Discrimination Act 1995
DWP	Department of Work and Pensions
EAT	Employment Appeal Tribunal
ECJ	European Court of Justice
EEA	European Economic Area
ERA	Employment Rights Act 1996
HMRC	Her Majesty's Revenue and Customs
HSE	Health and Safety Executive
LEL	Lower Earnings Limit
OMA	Occupational Medical Advisor
OSP	Occupational Sick Pay
RTW	Return-to-Work
SOSR	Some other substantial reason
SSP	Statutory Sick Pay
WTR	Working Time Regulations 1998

Contents

Foreword   xv

Preface   xvii

About Absence   1

Background   2

Reasons For Absence   5

Consider Prevention As Well As Cure   8

Absence Management Procedure   13

Patterns Of Absence   15

Methods Of Measuring Absence   17

Keeping Records   19

Implications Of The Data Protection Act 1998   21

Ensure Reporting Procedures Are Followed   23

Trigger Points   27

Return-To-Work Meetings   31

Points To Cover In A Return-To-Work Meeting   33

Return-To-Work Meeting Questions   36

The Headmistress Technique   38

Disability Discrimination   42

Matters To Consider In Reaching A Conclusion As To
Whether An Employee Is Disabled   48

Normal Day-To-Day Activities   56

Less Favourable Treatment   63

Reasonable Adjustments   67

Dealing With Persistent Short-Term Absence   72

Effective Strategies In Managing Short-Term
Absence   75

Disciplinary Action   79

Long-Term Sickness Absence   82

Dismissal For Capability   88

The Doctor Dilemma – Getting Medical Advice   91

Occupational Medical Advisor v Employee's
Own GP   94

Access To Medical Reports Act 1988   95

Conflicting Medical Reports   96

Workplace Stress   99

Reducing The Risk Of Stress   106

Handling Stress At Work   112

Introduction To SSP   119

Appendices

1 Health screening form   126

2 Sample absence management procedure   129

3.1 Letter to an employee who is refusing to talk
to you   138

3.2 Follow up letter to an employee who is
refusing to talk to you   140

4 Sample letter to doctor and health
questionnaire   142

5 Some key points from the Court of Appeal
in Hatton and others in 2002   145

Useful Contacts   147

Off the Sick List! training   148

Employment law training   149

Law on the Move   150

Foreword

Employment law? Let's not touch it - it's completely incomprehensible and prone to giving employers a real headache. Best leave it to the solicitors to unravel the murky depths of contracts, redundancy, maternity rights, capability and so on.

Or so I thought...

If you're like me, someone managing an organization and the people within it, you may well have thought that after the torrent of employment legislation in recent years, employers might just as well lie down in a darkened room and rely on luck. There are a lot of confused and nervous managers out there and no wonder. With so many changes in the legislation, a mass of case law (not always terribly helpful to us non-legal people) and an increasing number of employees who know their rights and are more than prepared to go to tribunal, the tendency to try and duck problems for an easy life is no great surprise. But we all know that ignoring a problem only makes it worse.

Management by crossing your fingers and praying *might* work, but I'd prefer not to leave things to chance. Fortunately, there are people out there like Kate Russell working to point us in the right direction. In *Off the Sick List!*, Kate shows us that being an employer really isn't as bad as all that. When approached correctly, with proper attention paid to the process and always taking care to record everything, she proves that employers *have* got rights and can manage fairly, lawfully and firmly.

This is a great book to learn from. After reading through the first few pages, I was convinced that by following the techniques discussed here I can ensure that the management reins are firmly in my hands. Kate is blessed with the rare ability to explain complicated material in simple, easy-to-understand English. She is practical, robust and experienced. The legal points are illustrated with case studies and examples, so that you not only know what to do, you also know how to do it.

Dealing with attendance is one of the last taboos for managers. We all know we have to do it, but it's often done more in a spirit of ticking off a checklist rather than really using it as an opportunity to tackle issues. Done like that it's a complete waste of time. Let's get brave and manage those with chronic Mondayitis! Let's make sure we fully consider all reasonable adjustments for employees who are long term sick to support them in their return to work. Properly applied these techniques increase productivity and profitability. In this book the process of tackling attendance is getting a boost. All employers will find this a beneficial read.

Bob Champion MBE

July 2008

Preface

It is a fact of life that people become ill from time to time. You very occasionally come across those rare employees who have never had taken a day's sickness absence in 20 years, but I can count the number of such hardy souls on the fingers of one hand and still have a few fingers left over. It's true that the more senior the role, the less sickness absence people tend to take, but even senior managers and self-employed people get sick occasionally (and their motivation to attend for work tends to be among the highest there is).

As employers we have to accept that there will always be some sickness absence and manage accordingly. There is a distinction between knowing that there will be some sickness absence and managing unacceptable levels. It's important to remember that life isn't always black and white and that while our policies and procedures provide useful guidance, there's no 'one size fits all approach'. Every case turns on its own facts.

That said, as employers we also have a responsibility to deal with absence. Absence can be a serious drain on a business for both large and small organizations, with the direct costs running to billions of pounds a year. Absence places a burden on colleagues and a failure to manage poor attendance can result in poor morale if the issue is not tackled, with a consequent effect on productivity and profitability.

Tackling absence isn't always straightforward. Absences come in many different forms, may be of varying durations and come about for a variety of reasons.

Employers have to develop a range of proportionate responses. There is no one 'right' way of going about it, but any actions you take must always be fair and reasonable. Remember that inappropriate or discriminatory action can lead to expensive legal settlements.

Many employers are reluctant to manage absence, but it's really important to take control of any attendance issues. The costs of absence are high and failure to address problems impacts on everyone in the business. Simple 'crack-downs' can be counter-productive, but attendance control works better where it is part of a wider set of measures. Dealing effectively with absence calls for a continuous and coordinated effort. Sound, fair and consistent policies and procedures can provide a framework within which absence problems can be better handled.

The real key to success to managing absence at work is taking action at an early stage, keeping good records and following correct procedures.

I hope that you'll find this book helpful in taking the right steps at the right time.

Kate Russell

August 2008

About Absence

According to the Confederation of British Industry (CBI), the estimated cost of sickness absence for UK businesses in 2006 was at least £13.4 billion (though some estimates put it significantly higher). Absences increased in 2006 as workers took an average of seven days off sick compared with 6.6 days the year before. This is calculated to have resulted in a total of 175 million lost working days.

At the company level, the costs of absence can be substantial. High absence levels tend to mean high overheads. Some indication of cost to the company is obtained simply by adding up the days of lost production and assessing the extra burden on the company's sick pay scheme.

There are other costs too.

- Unnecessarily high staffing levels and overtime payments.

- Replacement labour.

- Delayed production.

- Management time.

- Lower quality or levels of service.

- Disruption of the flow of work.

- Low morale and general dissatisfaction, resulting in good attenders leaving and/or low productivity.

Background

Absence levels across the UK are measured in two main ways.

Method one

Annual surveys conducted by CBI and the Chartered Institute of Personnel and Development (CIPD), asking organizations to estimate their sickness absence rates and the associated costs.

In 2007 the CBI/AXA Absence Survey reviewed sickness absence rates in more than 400 organizations. The following list sets out the key findings.

- Average absence increased from 6.6 days in 2005 to 7.0 days in 2006.

- In total 175 million working days were lost costing UK businesses over £13 billion.

- Manual workers were absent from work more often than non-manual employees.

- Manual workers recorded higher levels of absence (8.2 days) than their non-manual counterparts (5.7 days).

- Absence correlates with employer size, with the smallest employers (fewer than 50 employees) having half the absence rate of the largest ones (5000+ employees) - 4.0 days and 8.0 days, respectively.

- Public sector absence was 44 per cent higher than absence in the private sector.

- Long-term absence (20+ days) accounted for 43 per cent of working time lost, costing the UK economy £5.8 billion; it accounted for over half (52 per cent) of lost working time in the public sector compared with 38 per cent in the private sector.

- The chief causes of long term absence were stress, anxiety, depression and back pain.

The figures remain roughly the same from year to year and don't disclose any real surprises. The main area of change in recent years has been a steady growth in figures relating to stress, anxiety and depression.

Method two

Absence rates data is also collected by questioning individual employees through the General Household Survey and the Labour Force Survey. Estimates from the latter put the average absence rate somewhat lower than data collected by the CBI or CIPD, but it does confirm that rates of absence are higher in the public sector.

The strategies in the surveys that reportedly had the greatest impact were:

- waiting a period of days before paying sick pay;

- offering bonuses for good attendance;

- providing early access to medical care through private medical insurance.

Although there's no doubt that sickness absence results in billions of pounds of cost to employers, the results of the surveys referred to above should be treated with some caution, as several studies have indicated that data collection and analysis is flawed. Many employers do not have an accurate picture of the costs of sickness absence.

Costing sickness absence in the UK[1] was a study carried out in 2001. Seven organizations estimated that absence costs between two per cent and 16 per cent of annual salary costs, with only half of this being due to the direct costs of paying absent employees. The conclusion reached in this study was that even the most leading-edge UK employers appear fundamentally ill-equipped to form a view of their sickness absence costs. (IES Report, 2001).

In a further study, *How Employers Manage Absence*[2], a case study investigation of 13 organizations, the researchers found that in only two could managers place ny financial cost on absence (Bevan et al, DTI Employment Relations Research Series, 2004).

---

[1] Costing Sickness Absence in the UK, Bevan S, Hayday S, Report 382, Institute for Employment Studies, October 2001.

[2] How Employers Manage Absence, Bevan S, Dench S, Harper H, Hayday S, Employment Relations Research Series ERRS25, Department of Trade and Industry, March 2004.

Reasons For Absence

Not all absences are caused by sickness. There are several different reasons.

- Sickness absence (uncertificated, self-certificated or covered by a doctor's certificate).

- Unauthorised absence or persistent lateness.

- Other authorised absences: for example, statutory rights to leave (annual leave; maternity, paternity, adoption, or parental leave; time off for public or trade union duties; or to care for dependents) or contractual rights (compassionate leave).

Deal with unauthorised absence through the disciplinary process as it is a misconduct matter, but always investigate absences before reaching a conclusion. Remember there are many legitimate reasons why an employee might be absent.

The Employment Rights Act provides that employees must be given time off by their employers to attend public duties. This includes responsibilities like sitting as a magistrate, being a member of a local authority, policy authority, board of prison visitors or prison visiting committee. In terms of the amount of time allowed, there is no prescribed level but it must be 'reasonable in the circumstances'.

Example

R-W worked for A Ltd. She was appointed as a magistrate and her duties required her to sit for 13 days per year. A Ltd would only allow her five days' unpaid leave to attend to her public duties and told her to use her annual leave to cover the remaining eight days. R-W resigned and brought a claim of constructive dismissal and breach of her statutory right to take reasonable time off to attend public duties. Constructive dismissal arises where the employer fundamentally breaches the employment contract and the employee accepts the breach and resigns in response to it.

Initially, the employment tribunal held that A Ltd had not prevented the applicant taking time off to carry out her public duties and that her resignation did not amount to a constructive dismissal in the circumstances. R-W successfully appealed against this decision and the EAT said that the tribunal had failed to have proper regard to the provision of the Employment Rights Act covering time off for public duties. They said that the tribunal should not have considered whether time off was given, but rather whether the applicant was given 'a reasonable amount of time off', which should be assessed objectively with reference to the requirements of the particular public office held and the needs of the employer's business.

Riley-Williams v Argos Ltd [2003]

Many employers are unaware of their obligations in this area. There's no legal duty to do so but it's sensible to have a clear policy in place dealing with time off for public duties. Ensure that it is communicated to all staff and exercised consistently. When deciding what time off to allow an employee, look at matters objectively and consider both the demands of the business as well as the employee's position.

Consider Prevention As Well As Cure

Managing attendance starts at the recruitment stage. Try not to recruit a problem. I'm a firm believer that if an employee had chronic 'Mondayitis' in his last job, he'll go on having chronic 'Mondayitis' in this job (leopards don't change their spots) and that means all the pain and time of having to manage him. Minimize your risk by building in some checks, for example, using a health screening questionnaire (see an example at Appendix 1), testing and cross-checking information gathered during the recruitment process against references. You should only ask about conditions relevant to the particular job that you're advertising. For example, you might ask about arm or hand problems if the job requires frequent use of a keyboard. This means that you will have to change the form to meet the requirements of different jobs.

One of the most cost-effective ways of managing attendance is to try to prevent employees from being absent by tackling the underlying causes of absence in the first place.

Most people want to do a good job and will attend for work regularly. If they are motivated, interested in their work, feel that they are being fairly and equitably treated and reasonably rewarded, that their company is a good place to work and they have a sense of involvement, then most people are less likely to be absent.

There will always be some employees whose absence is unsatisfactory and whose attendance needs to be closely managed, but these incidences will usually decrease if you take good preventative action.

Some absence will be outside management's control, but levels of absence can be reduced when positive policies are introduced to improve working conditions and increase employees' motivation to attend work.

You could consider taking all or some of the following steps.

- Pre-employment health screening.

- Investigate how to improve physical working conditions.

- Offer healthy options in staff restaurants and at meetings.

- Investigate initiatives to promote a healthier workforce.

- Take ergonomic factors into account when designing workplaces.

- Ensure that health and safety standards are maintained.

- Give new starters, especially young people, sufficient training and ensuring that they receive particular attention during the initial period of their work.

- Wherever possible, design jobs so that they provide job satisfaction; jobs should provide variety, discretion, responsibility, contact with other people, feedback, some challenge and have clear goals.

- Review and update relevant policies, for example, training, career development and promotion policies, communication procedures and welfare provision to see if they can be improved.

- Ensure policies on equal opportunities and discrimination are fair and observed.

- Train managers so they can carry out their role properly and ensure they take an interest in their employees' health and welfare.

- Make confidential counselling services available for employees.

- Introduce flexible working hours or varied working arrangements, if this would assist employees without conflicting with production or other work demands.

- Encourage people to take their holidays within the prescribed period.

Where you offer permanent health insurance and healthcare schemes, ensure that these benefits are not withdrawn at the age of 60 or 65 (which is when the premiums tend to rise steeply). This would be direct discrimination under the age discrimination legislation. It's unlikely that a tribunal would accept the withdrawal of a benefit if cost alone is used as justification.

A failure to consider an employee's entitlements on termination for long-term sickness could result in an unfair dismissal. To avoid this situation, put in place a proper system for the management of long-term sickness absence to ensure that you take all the necessary steps before dismissal.

Example

H was a bus driver for FL. Following a suspected stroke in June and again in October 2005, he was signed off as unfit for work and his driving licence was withdrawn for a minimum of 12 months.

The company's sick pay scheme stated that where an employee was incapable of carrying out his role, the company would consider him for any other suitable employment. In the absence of such alternatives, he would be retired under the company pension scheme as being incapable of efficiently discharging his duties and certified as permanently incapable of doing so. Alternatively, he would be dismissed on medical grounds.

H's manager considered that H's ill health was not permanent and decided that H should be dismissed on the ground of incapability, or alternatively go on the holding register (for which there was no sick pay). H initially went onto the register, but disagreed that his sick pay should end. He was dismissed.

He appealed and the company sought further medical information from H's specialist.

At his appeal, relying on only the occupational health advice that his condition could not be considered permanent, H was given the choice of being dismissed or remaining on the books with sick pay extended for a few months, before going onto the holding register and retiring with no application for an ill-health pension. H refused to accept the company's terms and was dismissed. He successfully claimed unfair dismissal.

On appeal, the EAT agreed that H's dismissal was unfair.

The company had not taken reasonable steps before his dismissal. Reasonable steps include consulting with the employee, taking medical advice and considering alternative employment. Where the employer provides an ill-health retirement pension, it should also take reasonable steps to ascertain a long-term sick employee's entitlement to that benefit, which includes seeking medical advice.

The company had failed to honour its own sick pay scheme, which stated that it would consider ill-health retirement along with termination on medical grounds, but also that it was 'good industrial practice' to consider ill-health retirement where this forms part of the employee's benefits package. The requirement for an ill-health retirement application to be signed off by a medical adviser meant that the company had an essential role in ensuring that retirement was considered before dismissal.

First West Yorkshire Ltd t/a First Leeds v Haigh [2008]

Absence Management Procedure

Managing absence certainly takes some effort and is often unpopular with line managers.

In most companies the main problem is persistent short term absence and managers sometimes feel overwhelmed by the volume of work it creates. It's worth remembering that most staff do make the effort to come to work most of the time and want to do a good job. They also want their manager to manage those employees who have chronic 'Mondayitis'. Their view is "why should we carry this person?". If the manager doesn't tackle matters effectively, good staff often vote with their feet and leave.

The good news is that consistent effort will bring about and maintain improvements. Consistency is the key to success, so you really have to stick at it. Good absence management takes a joint approach involving HR, line managers and medical advisors to make it work most effectively.

The starting point is to clearly set out the company's standards and what will happen if they are not met. An example is shown in the Sample Absence Management Procedure at Appendix 2.

HR support will largely be based around providing support, guidance and advice to line managers. This function may also be used to coordinate the company's approach and may carry out the monitoring of absence on a central basis.

Line managers are generally the first point of contact when employees call in sick. They have to manage the absence by keeping records, rescheduling work and conducting return-to-work (RTW) interviews.

Medical advisors will be used to advise on the state of the employee's health and the likely prognosis, as well as giving guidance as to what the employer can do to make adjustments to support the employee.

Patterns Of Absence

There are a number of variables associated with patterns of absence, such as management style, traditions of behaviour and working conditions. Research has identified that these patterns often display a number of common features.

- Young people tend to have more frequent sickness absences than older people, but the length of the absences tend to be shorter.

- The most likely periods for absence are Mondays, Fridays, before or after a bank holiday, along with late shifts.

- Manual employees generally have higher levels of absence than office employees.

- Unauthorised absence is more common among new starters; longer serving employees get to know the organization's standards and stay within the framework.

- Absences can sometimes relate to annual events: such as school holidays, public holidays or major sporting occasions.

- Sick leave due to industrial accidents is also greater for new or inexperienced employees.

- Absence tends to increase where there are high levels of overtime or frequently rotating shift patterns.

- Absence is likely to be greater in larger companies.

Methods Of Measuring Absence

There are a number of different ways in which organizations can define and measure absence.

1. The most common measure of absence is the lost time rate. This shows the percentage of the total time available which has been lost because of absence from all causes in a given period.

The lost time rate is regarded as an overall measure of the severity of the problem. If calculated separately by department or group of employees, it can show up particular problem areas.

Total time lost may consist of a small number of people who are absent for long periods, or a large number absent for short spells.

Lost time rate =

Total absence in the period) x 100
Possible total (of working days or hours)

2. You may want to asses the measure of frequency to show how widespread the problem is within the business. The frequency rate shows the average number of spells of absence per employee (expressed as a percentage) irrespective of the length of each spell.

Frequency rate =

No of spells of absence in period x 100
No of employees in the period

3. If you want to monitor the number of employees absent during the period, the individual frequency rate can be used.

Individual frequency rate =

No employees having 1 or more absence spells x 100
No of employees

Keeping Records

You must have a system for recording absence, or it will not only be impossible to measure specific types, such as long-term sickness absence, but also to notice when trigger points have been reached. Without the information to indicate the scale of the problem, you won't be able to manage the situation effectively. This means that employees need to know what you expect of them. For instance, the correct reporting procedures, what documentation they're expected to complete and what information they should submit.

Note that you're also under a legal duty to keep records of SSP for HMRC (see Introduction to SSP on page 119).

Some companies create and publish league tables to compare absence data emerging from different departments or sites. These can prove a useful reminder to managers and provide information which can be used in review meetings.

One of the chief advantages of objective measurement and analysis of absence is the correction or confirmation of subjective views.

The sort of questions you might usefully ask yourself are listed below.

- Is there really a problem?

- Which sections or shifts are affected?

- Are particular groups affected, such as one sex or ethnic minority?

- Does the problem extend throughout the whole organization or is it confined to one or two departments or functions?

- How many employees are involved? Is it only a few or a large number, indicating a general problem?

- What type of absence is involved? Are they mainly certificated absences or many cases of one-day absences or lateness?

If you want to compare your company's absence rate with that of other companies in the industry or geographical area, (to see if you've got a problem and if so how serious it is), then you may be able to obtain figures for other organizations through local employers' groups. National surveys of absence are carried out periodically by bodies such as the CBI and the Work Foundation.

Another source of information is The Labour Force Survey, prepared by the Office for National Statistics (www.statistics.gov.uk), which provides information about employees' absences from work caused by sickness or injury.

Implications Of The Data Protection Act 1998

The general principles of data collected under the Data Protection Act place a duty on employers to ensure that they collect and process data appropriately. This means that you should not collect more data than is reasonably necessary or relevant for the purpose, ensure that it is held securely and is only used for the purpose for which it is collected.

Data relating to the reasons for sickness absence is sensitive personal data, which means that you can only collect and process such data if you have express (i.e. written) informed permission from the employee.

Please note that provided the above guidelines are followed it is quite acceptable to ask for relevant medical information prior to employment.

Part 2 of the Code of Practice dealing with employment records suggests that absence records should be kept separately from sickness records which contain the details of the absences.

Part 4 of the Code dealing with medical records and health information established the general principle that you should only collect information relating to the health of individual employees if:

- express, freely given consent has been provided by the employee(s) concerned; or

- the collection is necessary to enable compliance with the employer's legal obligations (for example, to prevent breaching the health and safety regulations and/or anti-discrimination rules).

Collection of medical records and health information relating to individual employees not covered by the above is likely to be unlawful and a breach of the Act.

Ensure Reporting Procedures Are Followed

There should be clear procedures for employees to follow when they are advising you of their absence. Decide on the procedures you wish to adopt and communicate them to your staff. The sort of areas you should cover are listed below.

- The person from whom you will accept a notification of sickness.

- The manager or supervisor to whom the absence should be reported.

- The time by which the notification should be made.

- What information you need to ensure you have up-to-date knowledge of the absence and for use in the RTW meeting.

When I write terms and conditions of employment for companies I tend to spell out that the communication must normally be made by phone by the sick employee. I don't accept text messages or emails (if someone is well enough to text me they're probably well enough to phone me). I also say that it is the employee's responsibility to ensure that he has the means to contact the employer; that includes having enough credit on his mobile phone.

The general rule is that employees should make the call in person. Encourage your employees to stick to the reporting requirements. In most cases there will be no reason why the employee can't comply. Research shows that the vast majority of time taken off as sickness absence is short term and for very minor illnesses (coughs, colds etc), very few of which preclude the use of a phone.

Where there are exceptional circumstances and the employee can't call in person (for example, the employee's in casualty waiting to have a broken leg set), it's a good idea to find out what the situation is and whether you can do anything to help out.

In reality, companies often allow a third party to call on behalf of the sick employee. It's not a satisfactory arrangement, nor is it a good idea to allow messages to be taken by switchboards or left on an answer phone. Managing absence is about managing employees on a person-to-person basis.

For many busy managers, this is a responsibility that arises at the start of the day when they're trying to deal with lots of other pressing matters. It might be worth training a nominated person to take such calls.

Use telephone conversations positively. When a sick employee phones in, take down as much information as you can. Prepare a template to ensure that you collect all the relevant data. Always be firm, polite and sensitive. However tempting, don't indulge in robust expressions of doubt as to the truthfulness of the reported illness!

Make arrangements to make contact later in the day (or the following day) for a progress report so that you can plan for the following day.

Ask:

- What is wrong with the employee?

- What are the symptoms?

- When did he first experience the symptoms?

- What's the employee doing about seeking medical advice? Get as much detail as you can.

Make a note of the date and time of the telephone call to ensure that your reporting procedures have been followed.

Where it appears that someone is not being strictly truthful with you, it's surprising how often a later conversation varies factually from an earlier conversation. Employees engaging in such tactics can't recall accurately what they've said to you and it is these discrepancies we should gently explore and question.

You can use this data in the RTW meeting.

Case study

Catering firm Brakes Group supplies food to the catering industry in the UK and France. It has more than 7,000 employees in 70 locations. A new programme was introduced to cover approximately 4,500 operational employees, principally in warehouse and driving jobs. The nature of the company's activities meant that the absence of staff such as drivers was felt immediately and cover would be required at short notice.

Brakes decided to change its approach to managing absence early in 2005. Absence was running at about six per cent before the programme started.

The company has outsourced the recording and management of routine unplanned absence. Absent employees now call Brakes Healthline, a nurse-based helpline run by Active Health Partners. There is someone available on the Healthline 24 hours a day. The nurse discusses the absence and arranges a follow-up at a pre-agreed time with the employee to offer medical advice and support. Included in the discussion is an estimate as to when the employee is likely to be back at work. The nurse informs the line manager and manages the absence from this point.

Employees benefit from easy access to a free, confidential health advice. Brakes Group's management team will have access to online information from a central database, enabling them to understand issues and measure the impact of health and safety improvement initiatives. This means that line managers can concentrate on managing attendance when a trigger mechanism suggests there may be a problem.

Absence figures have been reduced to around 3.5 %.

Trigger Points

Many companies now have a point at which concern is formally triggered and which suggests that an employee's attendance requires review. The trigger point is determined by the individual business. You can set very high standards, but remember that these are always open to the overriding requirement of reasonableness.

I've lost count of the number of managers who have confessed to me that they haven't managed an employee with a poor attendance record, because the employee in question is so good when he does appear. The point is to encourage the employee to appear for work consistently and perform well throughout.

When I'm delivering training I often mention the persistent short-term offenders who cause the most pain to the business. It's always the same people. Most companies have a few and you'll know who they are in your business.

When should you take action? Well, there is no legal standard of attendance. It comes down to your own organization's standards. Some companies use a certain number of periods of absence in a specific timescale as a trigger, such as five or more absences in any 12-month period.

Others use the Bradford Factor. This formula can be useful for revealing staff with high levels of short-term absence. Certain types of absence should be excluded from this calculation, for example, absences related to pregnancy, disability or underlying illness.

The Bradford Factor is useful in identifying persistent short-term offenders. The formula is:

(number of episodes)^2 x total days off

Using this formula, persistent short-term offenders can be clearly highlighted. For example:

- One absence of five days in a given period = Bradford Factor 5 (one episode x one episode x 5)

- Five absences of one day in a given period = Bradford Factor 125 (5 episodes x 5 episodes x 5)

Different employers have formulated their own triggers.

Example

At British Airways the triggers encompass a number of different patterns of absence. These are:

- two or more occasions of absence in any rolling three-month period; or

- the loss of 4.5 per cent of working time in a rolling 12 month period; or

- an absence which exceeds 21 consecutive days.

The trigger you choose will depend on the capabilities of your recording and monitoring systems.

Triggers may be tied to a specific stage in the absence procedure, for example, informal counselling or a formal warning. The aim is to encourage improvement whilst imposing effective sanctions. It is usual to agree attendance targets at this point. If the target is not met, then disciplinary action usually follows.

It is important to put a specific figure on the improvement required and not just talk vaguely about improvement. You are always subject to the overriding requirement of reasonableness.

Example

A manager interviewed a female employee about her appalling attendance record. The manager pointed out that Doris' attendance record was unacceptably poor and that she had taken 20 sick days in the last three months. He asked Doris to make an effort to improve her attendance and advised her that if she did not do so he would have to take her through the disciplinary process for non-attendance and she might ultimately be dismissed. Doris listened carefully and agreed to all this.

Three months later they met again. The manager discovered that she had indeed improved – she had taken a mere 16 days of sickness absence, instead of 20. So he got what he **asked for**, not what he **wanted**.

What he should have said was something along the lines of "If you are off work more than two days during the next three months, I will talk to you again as part of our formal disciplinary procedure."

Note that where an employee is clearly making strenuous efforts to attend work and he is ill with a genuine illness during the review period, it wouldn't be reasonable to immediately enter into formal disciplinary action. You have to demonstrate reasonableness and some flexibility. Exercise your management discretion, continue monitoring and act accordingly.

To avoid confusion and disputes, it is sensible to have a clear-cut written procedure for absence management. There is no legal standard for identifying and dealing with short-term absentees, but remember that the employer is always subject to the over-riding requirement of reasonableness.

Return-To-Work Meetings

The RTW meeting developed during the 1980s when self-certification of short absences was introduced, with the result that firms were encouraged to review this process rather than simply rely on a doctor's note.

Used as part of a wider attendance management process, RTW meetings are one of the most effective ways of reducing persistent short-term sickness and can help identify short-term absence problems at an early stage. They also provide an opportunity to start discussing issues which might be causing the absence.

Carry out RTW meetings with all employees returning from sickness absence, however short or long the absence. It avoids accusations that you are picking on an individual and it gives you the opportunity to pick up on potential problems before they develop into something much more serious.

Although this is one of the best tools you can use, it has to be done properly. Some managers feel very uncomfortable having this conversation, even though it's part and parcel of their job. They *hate* saying "we've missed you" (too pink and fluffy!), and all the other things that go with attendance management. This discomfort manifests itself in several ways.

- Poor eye contact (many become fascinated with the papers on their desk or the toe of their shoe).

- Failing to probe properly or at all.

- Failing to agree specific improvement targets.

- Others say that they're only doing it because "HR have told them to".

I do despair sometimes!

If you fall into either of these categories, you are missing an opportunity. You don't have to be pink and fluffy you can find your own style. But you *do* have to carry out this meeting correctly, otherwise all you'll be doing is ticking off a checklist. It will have no impact and is waste of everyone's time.

RTW meetings are a golden opportunity to:

- welcome back those employees whose attendance is normally satisfactory and to thank them for their commitment to the organization; and

- start to move those whose attendance is poor out of their comfort zone by calling them to account.

Points To Cover In A Return-To-Work Meeting

Always carry out RTW meetings in private. This is mostly to ensure that you protect the employee's confidential information. The other advantage is that it will prevent employees (who are so inclined) from playing to the gallery.

Use the meeting to complete or sign off any self-certification forms or to collect a doctor's certificate. The completion of a self-certification form is an ideal trigger point for a return-to-work discussion. Make sure you hold the meeting in private and preferably before the employee starts work on the day of return.

The meeting will go one of two ways, depending on the employee's attendance record.

1. Where an employee has generally good attendance, there are still points to be discussed.

- Welcome the employee back.

- Ask him how he is and confirm the reason for his absence.

- Ask whether medical advice has been sought or taken, if this is appropriate.

- Ask whether you need to take any actions to help him reintegrate into work.

- Use the meeting to update the employee with job-related information – what happened while he was off sick – and let him know that he was missed.

- Use the opportunity to thank the employee for his good attendance.

- Update your documentation.

Sometimes, employees are so conscientious that they will come back to work too early and may still be ill. In these circumstances, send them home again until they are recovered.

2. Where you have concerns about an employee's levels of attendance, the format will be rather different.

- Welcome the employee back.

- Ask him how he is and confirm the reason for the absence.

- Show him his attendance record and discuss the facts. Quite often the employee won't realise how much time he's had off and this reminder is all it takes.

- Ask whether medical advice has been sought or taken, if this is appropriate.

- Agree actions to reintegrate into work.

- Use the meeting to update the employee with job-related information – what happened while he was off sick. Let him know that he was missed.

- Ask the employee what can be done to improve his attendance, what you can reasonably do to help him achieve these improvements and agree specific improvements (we don't want a Doris scenario). Try to get his commitment.

- Update your documentation. Set a reasonable timescale (8-12 weeks) to review progress.

- Follow up at the due date.

It may be the case that the employee becomes angry or defensive and accuses you of suggesting that he's not been genuinely ill. Illness is not the issue here. The issue here is his attendance, about which you have concerns.

Return-To-Work Meeting Questions

Depending on the circumstances, here are some useful questions that may reasonably be asked. They won't all be appropriate in all circumstances.

- How have you been?

- What were the symptoms?

- When did you first notice the symptoms?

- What impact did the symptoms have on you?

- Are you struggling to do certain things? If so, what are they?

- What do you think caused them?

- Is there any underlying cause for your ill health absences (i.e. condition connecting the absences)?

- What medical advice did you seek?

- What does your doctor say?

- Are you being referred to a consultant (or other specialist)?

- If so, when is that likely to happen?

- What medication are you taking?

- Are there any side effects which might impact on your ability to carry out your duties?

- What level of work can you now undertake?

- How can I/we help you?

- Are there any reasonable adjustments we need to consider making?

- Are there any adjustments we haven't yet made which would help you?

- What are you doing to assist your recovery/ reduce the risk of repetition?

- What issues are there to be dealt with when you return to work?

- What would make it easier for you to come to work?

Sometimes you'll have someone in front of you and you have very good grounds for belief that he is a lead-swinger. No matter what the provocation, don't be sarcastic or flippant; this means not saying or asking the following ....

- You've been skiving again

- Good holiday?

- Don't worry – it's not a big problem (it is!)

- A few days' sickness is OK (it is not!)

- Just sort it out!

The Headmistress Technique

If you are dealing with an employee who has chronic 'Mondayitis', it's useful to adopt 'the headmistress technique' (or headmaster technique depending on your gender). I've been teased so much over the years about being rather headmistressy that I thought it was time to turn it to good account (my philosophy being if life hands you a lemon, make lemonade and sell it).

This is all about moving an employee out of his comfort zone gently, fairly, firmly, ethically and lawfully. You want your recalcitrant employee to think twice about coming in front of you. Here are some tips for asserting your authority in a gentle but very firm way.

- Wear formal clothing that is consistent with your work culture.

- Make sure the meeting is held in private.

- Tone and speed are important. Talk quietly, calmly and slowly. Pause to reflect from time to time. We're not used to gaps in conversation in our culture and silence can be very powerful if you have the courage to use it.

- Listen hard. That means checking your understanding by asking clarifying questions, making a few notes, summarising back what you think the employee is saying. It also means listening between the lines, i.e. what is the employee *not* saying. Never interrupt.

- Beam amiably (but not idiotically) at the employee as you chat through the reasons for his absence.

- Probe into all his statements using open questions, so that you have the fullest possible grasp of his explanation. Most managers don't probe and only take things at face value. You'll miss a lot if you don't probe carefully.

- It also means that if you have all the information you can back him into a corner, leaving him little choice but to agree to adhere to your standards.

- Make careful notes of what the employee says and any agreed actions. Taking notes helps you remember accurately what's been said, but it also sends a message to the employee that you are taking things very seriously.

- Where there is a pattern of absence, show the record to the employee and ask, "You've had five absences this year and four of them have been Mondays. Help me understand what's happening here", then wait for an answer.

- Sometimes it's enough just to show the attendance record to the employee and he gasps and says 'I haven't taken that much time off' and you beam a bit more, looking over the top of your reading glasses (a very effective little bit of theatre) and say "I *know* – it looks bad, doesn't it. I had to double check, but it is correct. You have the *worst attendance* in the department ..."

- Reiterate that you want to help and support the employee and will do everything you reasonably can, but he must meet you half-way. Only he can attend and that is what you want him to commit to do.

- We want our employees to be happy and successful at work. I say this and it appears in my notes just in case a tribunal ever gets to see them. It might sound a bit cheesey, but it doesn't stop it being true. I'd much rather fix a problem than dismiss and start again. It makes sense to think holistically.

- I also tend to have a bank of information about alternative therapies and remedies to hand, for example, information about local yoga classes, meditation tapes, Neuro-Linguistic Programming (NLP) and Emotional Freedom Techniques (EFT) websites. Sometimes employees have family or money difficulties, so for example I will take steps to help, such as making an appointment with a debt counsellor. We will do what it takes to get things moving in the right direction. On one occasion I had to help a man who was depressed, in part because of his weight. He had done nothing about it and had been complaining comfortably for some time that he practically lived on lettuce leaves (while scoffing HobNobs). At our meeting he (reluctantly) agreed to enrol as a member of a slimming group and I offered to drive him there for the first class. He was quite horrified by my helpfulness, but he went and once he got started he did lose about two stone and looked and felt far better.

- If you are putting in a review date, get out your diary there and then and still peering over your glasses, go through and put a suitable review date in. It's another little bit of theatre, another little message for the employee that this isn't going to go away. It works beautifully.

- Write to him with a summary of the conversation and agreements, including the review date.

I have adopted some or all of these tactics where I've had an employee with persistent short term absence and it works. (If you think you might need a bit of help to hone your headmistress technique, see the training section in the Additional Resources on page 147). In some cases, employees do shape up and start coming to work regularly. In others, where an employee has no intention of adhering to the standards he realises that the time has come for him to move on. Occasionally I have to manage someone through the full process, but it's less often than you might think.

Disability Discrimination

When you're dealing with sickness absence you have to be mindful of the requirements placed on employers by the Disability Discrimination Act 1995 (DDA).

According to research, around one in five people of working age are considered by the Government and by the Equality and Human Rights Commission (EHRC) to be disabled within the meaning of the DDA. If a person with a disability suffers unlawful discrimination in the workplace he can complain to the tribunal. There is no upper limit on compensation for discrimination, so an employer's unjustified discrimination, or failure to make reasonable adjustments, can be extremely costly.

You should not treat a disabled employee or disabled job applicant less favourably, for a reason relating to the disability, than others to whom that reason does not apply, unless that reason is material to the particular circumstances and substantial in nature. If the reason is both material and substantial, you may have to make a reasonable adjustment to reduce or remove it.

The definition of a disability under the DDA is 'a physical or mental impairment which has a substantial and long term adverse effect on his ability to carry out normal day-to-day activities.'

In order to fall within the DDA's definition of disabled a person must have a physical or mental impairment. In many cases, there will be no dispute about the existence of an impairment. Any disagreement is more likely to be about whether the effects of the impairment fall within the definition. Even so, it may sometimes be necessary to decide whether a person has an impairment, so as to be able to deal with issues about its effects. If in doubt, it's probably best to work on the basis that he has got a disability.

Impairment is interpreted very broadly and includes damage, defect, disorder or disease.

Whether a person is disabled for the purposes of the Act is generally determined by considering the effect that the impairment has on that person's ability to carry out normal day-to-day activities.

Many illnesses and conditions are capable of being disabilities within the meaning of the DDA. Whether they are found to be so by the court will depend on the circumstances. Only a few will automatically be considered to be disabilities (see page 45).

A disability can arise from a wide range of impairments. Listed below are some examples of conditions that the courts have found are capable of being disabilities.

- Sensory impairments, such as those affecting sight or hearing.

- Impairments with fluctuating or recurring effects such as rheumatoid arthritis, myalgic encephalitis (ME)/chronic fatigue syndrome (CFS), fibromyalgia, depression and epilepsy.

- Progressive disorders, such as motor neurone disease, muscular dystrophy, forms of dementia and lupus (SLE).

- Organ specific, for example, respiratory conditions, asthma, cardiovascular diseases, including thrombosis, stroke and heart disease.

- Developmental disorders, such as autistic spectrum disorders (ASD), dyslexia and dyspraxia.

- Learning difficulties.

- Mental health conditions and mental illnesses, such as depression, schizophrenia, eating disorders, bipolar affective disorders, obsessive compulsive disorders, as well as personality disorders and some self-harming behaviour.

- Club foot.

- Back injury (soft back tissue).

- Photosensitive epilepsy.

- Cerebral palsy;

- Diabetes;

- Migrainous neuralgia.

It may not always be possible to categorise a condition as either a physical or a mental impairment. The underlying cause of the impairment may be hard to establish and there may be adverse effects which are both physical and mental in nature. Sometimes effects of a mainly physical nature may stem from an underlying mental impairment and vice versa.

The cause of an impairment isn't relevant, even if it's a consequence of a condition which is excluded. For example, liver disease as a result of alcohol dependency would be an impairment, although alcoholism itself is expressly excluded from the scope of the DDA's definition of disability. What is important is the effect of the impairment, provided that it is not an excluded condition.

Certain conditions are deemed to meet the definition of disability from the date of diagnosis. These are cancer, HIV infection or multiple sclerosis (MS).

A person who is certified as blind or partially sighted by a consultant ophthalmologist, or is registered as such with a local authority will be regarded as disabled.

Severe disfigurements such as visible skin disease, scars and birthmarks, limb or postural deformation will usually be regarded as a disability. Not all disfigurements will be considered severe. Whether or not they are severe may depend partly on where they are on the body; for example a birthmark on the back may not be a severe disfigurement, whereas a similar mark on the employee's face might be considered severe. Having said that, disfigurements which consist of a tattoo (which has not been removed), non-medical body piercing, or something attached through such piercing, will not be regarded as a disability.

Certain conditions are specifically excluded from the DDA.

The exclusions are set out below.

- Addiction to, or dependency on, alcohol, nicotine, or any other substance (other than the result of the substance being medically prescribed).

- Seasonal allergic rhinitis (e.g. hay fever), except where it aggravates the effect of another condition.

- Tendency to set fires.

- tendency to steal;

- Tendency to physical or sexual abuse of other persons.

- Exhibitionism.

- Voyeurism.

Interestingly, a person with an excluded condition may enjoy the DDA's protection if he has an accompanying impairment which meets the requirements of the definition. For example, a person who is addicted to a substance such as alcohol may also have depression, or a physical impairment such as liver damage, arising from the alcohol addiction. While this person would not meet the definition simply on the basis of having an addiction, he may still meet the definition as a result of the effects of the depression or the liver damage.

Example

P was an alcoholic. She was diagnosed as suffering with depression. She was signed off sick for over one year and was eventually dismissed. She complained unsuccessfully in the first instance of disability discrimination.

There had been some debate between the parties as to whether the alcoholism was the cause or a symptom of the depression. On appeal, the EAT held that the cause of the depression was not relevant when deciding whether or not someone was disabled within the meaning of the DDA. The correct approach was to look at whether the impairment fell within the definition of 'disability' under the DDA and then look at whether the condition fell within one of the exclusions.

Power v Panasonic [2003]

Someone who is no longer disabled, but who met the requirements of the definition in the past, will still be covered by the Act. For example, a person who experienced a mental illness that had a substantial and long-term adverse effect on his ability to carry out normal day-to-day activities four years ago, but who has experienced no recurrence of the condition, is still entitled to the protection afforded by DDA, as a person with a past disability.

Matters To Consider In Reaching A Conclusion As To Whether An Employee Is Disabled

Where the disabled person is having treatment or correction, you have to consider what effect the impairment would have on the employee if he was not being treated (you'll probably need medical advice to determine this). The treatment or correction measures which are to be disregarded include medical treatment, including counselling and the use of a prosthesis or other aid.

This rule applies even if the measures result in the effects being completely under control or not at all apparent. Where treatment is continuing it may be having the effect of masking a disability, so that it does not have a substantial adverse effect. If the final outcome of such treatment cannot be determined or if it is known that removal of the medical treatment would result in either a relapse or a worsened condition, then you should disregard the medical treatment.

For example, in the case of someone with diabetes which is being controlled by medication or diet, or the case of a person with depression which is being treated by counselling, the decision whether or not the effect is substantial should be made by considering what the effects of the condition would be if he was not taking that medication or receiving counselling.

The exception to this situation is visual impairments where they are capable of being corrected by spectacles or contact lenses.

You must also take account of the effect of the continuing medical treatment where it creates a permanent, rather than a temporary improvement.

In deciding whether an employee is disabled, you have to consider whether his condition has an adverse impact on his day-to-day activities. The adverse effect must be a substantial one. This means it must be more than a condition which may be considered to be minor or trivial.

In determining whether or not the impairment is substantial, there are a number of factors to consider.

1. Time taken to carry out an activity

The time taken by a person with an impairment to carry out a normal day-to-day activity may be relevant when assessing whether the impairment's effect is substantial. Compare it with the time it might take a person who does not have the impairment to complete an activity.

Another factor is the way in which a person with that impairment carries out a normal day-to-day activity, compared with the way that the person might be expected to carry out the activity if he does not have the impairment.

2. Cumulative effects of the impairment

Taken in isolation an impairment might not have a substantial adverse effect on a person's ability to undertake a particular day-to-day activity, but its effects on more than one activity taken together, could result in an overall substantial adverse effect.

For example, a person whose impairment causes breathing difficulties may as a result experience minor effects on the ability to carry out a number of activities such as getting washed and dressed, preparing a meal, or travelling on public transport. But taken together, the cumulative result would amount to a substantial adverse effect on his ability to carry out these normal day-to-day activities.

3. Environmental factors

Environmental conditions may exacerbate the effect of an impairment. Factors such as temperature, humidity, lighting, the time of day or night, how tired the person is, or how much stress he is under, may have an impact on the effects. When assessing whether adverse effects are substantial you should consider the extent to which such environmental factors are likely to exacerbate the effects.

The focus here is on what the worker cannot do or can only do with difficulty. Just because the employee can carry out a number of day-to-day activities doesn't mean that he is not substantially affected.

Example

G was a paranoid schizophrenic. He coped adequately with living alone. However, his evidence was that he suffered from hallucinations, had difficulty concentrating and misinterpreted the words of his work colleagues in a paranoid way. In addition, he was unable to hold a normal conversation, behaved strangely at times and had significantly impaired concentration.

The EAT found that the symptoms of his illness impaired his ability to concentrate and communicate and that did affect his ability to carry out normal, day-to-day activities substantially.

Goodwin v Patent Office [1999]

4. Effects of behaviour

In deciding what is substantial, consider how far a person can reasonably be expected to modify his behaviour to prevent or reduce the effects of an impairment on normal day-to-day activities. If he can reasonably be expected to behave in such a way that the effect of the impairment doesn't have a substantial adverse effect on his ability to carry out normal day-to-day activities then he would no longer meet the definition of disability. For example, when considering modification of behaviour, it would be reasonable to expect a person who has back pain to avoid extreme activities such as parachuting. It would not be reasonable to expect him to give up or modify more normal activities that might exacerbate the symptoms, such as moderate gardening, shopping or using public transport.

You also have to take into account a situation where a person avoids doing things, which for example, cause pain, fatigue or substantial social embarrassment because of a loss of energy and motivation. It wouldn't be reasonable to conclude that a person who employed an avoidance strategy was not a disabled person. In determining whether a person meets the definition of disability it is important to consider the things that a person cannot do, or can only do with difficulty, rather than focussing on those things that a person can do.

For example an employee with a persistent stammer may use coping strategies to manage his condition, such as avoiding using the telephone, not giving verbal instructions at work or limiting social contact outside his immediate family. It may not be immediately apparent that he has an impairment which adversely affects his ability to carry out normal day-to-day activities.

In determining whether he meets the definition of disability, think about the extent to which it is reasonable to expect him to place such restrictions on his working and domestic life.

Special conditions apply to progressive conditions such as systemic lupus erythematosis (SLE), various types of dementia, rheumatoid arthritis and motor neurone disease.

A person with a progressive condition should be treated as having an impairment which substantially affects him from the moment the condition from which he suffers causes him to experience difficulties in carrying out normal day-to-day activities. This is subject to the proviso that in the future the adverse effect is more likely than not to become substantial. In most cases this will have to be established through the medical route. Note that the effect need not be continuous and need not be substantial. The person will still need to show that the impairment meets the requirements of 'long-term'.

A person with a progressive condition which has no effect on day-to-day activities because it has been successfully treated (for example by surgery) may still have a disability where the effects of that treatment give rise to a further impairment which does have an effect on normal day-to-day activities. For example, the treatment of a condition may result in an impairment adversely impacts on normal day-to-day activities and the impairment's effects are likely to become substantial in the future.

The definition of impairment is sufficiently flexible to include a condition which has come about as a result of medical treatment.

Example

K had treatment for prostate cancer and as a result developed minor incontinence. The court held that the impairment was sufficiently closely linked to the condition treated to result from it and was therefore a disability.

Kirton v Tetrosyl Ltd [2003]

For the purpose of deciding whether a person is disabled, a long-term effect of an impairment is one:

- which has lasted at least 12 months; or

- where the total period for which it lasts, from the time of the first onset, is likely to be at least 12 months; or

- which is likely to last for the rest of the life of the person affected.

The effects of an impairment don't have to be active all the time for the impairment to qualify as a disability. If the impairment has had a substantial adverse effect on a person's ability to carry out normal day-to-day activities, but that effect stops or is not always apparent, the substantial effect is regarded as continuing if it is likely to recur. (In deciding whether a person has had a disability in the past, the question is whether a substantial adverse effect has in fact recurred.) Conditions with effects which recur only sporadically, or for short periods, can still qualify as impairments for the purposes of the Act, in respect of the meaning of 'long-term'

The type of conditions with effects which can recur, or where effects can be sporadic, include rheumatoid arthritis, Menières disease and epilepsy as well as mental health conditions such as schizophrenia, bipolar affective disorder, and certain types of depression. (The Regulations specifically exclude hay fever, except where it aggravates the effects of an existing condition.) These are only examples and it is not intended to be an exhaustive list.

Some impairments with recurring or fluctuating effects may be less obvious in their impact on the individual concerned. They will still be considered to be impairments.

If medical or other treatment is likely to permanently cure a condition and therefore remove the impairment, so that recurrence of its effects would then be unlikely even if there were no further treatment, consider this when looking at the likelihood of recurrence of those effects. However, if the treatment simply delays or prevents a recurrence and a recurrence would be likely if the treatment stopped, as is the case with most medication, then the treatment is to be ignored and the effect is to be regarded as likely to recur.

Normal Day-To-Day Activities

An impairment is to be taken to affect the ability of a person to carry out normal day-to-day activities only if it affects that person in respect of one or more of the following:

- mobility;

- manual dexterity;

- physical co-ordination;

- continence;

- ability to lift, carry or otherwise move everyday objects;

- speech, hearing or eyesight;

- memory or ability to concentrate, learn or understand; or

- perception of the risk of physical danger.

Note that this list is *not* a list of day-to-day activities because it's not feasible to provide an exhaustive list.

Day-to-day activities cover the things people do on a regular or daily basis. Guidance is given by the courts. Examples include shopping, reading and writing, having a conversation or using the telephone, watching television, getting washed and dressed, preparing and eating food, carrying out household tasks, walking and travelling by various forms of transport and taking part in social activities. Sports and leisure pursuits are *not* included.

Example

S started work with CCE as a warehouseman in November 1999. As a result of an accident that S claimed that he suffered at work in December 1999 he was absent from work for almost a year. On 25 October 2000 he was dismissed on the grounds of incapability. He bought a claim before the employment tribunal that his dismissal amounted to disability discrimination.

In order to establish that he had a disability S gave examples of how his back condition impacted on his day-to-day activities, citing cycling, keeping goal and playing snooker. The court found that it was not sufficient to demonstrate a substantial adverse impact on normal day-to-day activities under the DDA. Sports, hobbies and games are not to be treated as normal day-to-day activities for the purposes of the Act.

Coca Cola Enterprises v Shergill [2003]

'Normal' does not include activities which are normal only for a particular person, or a small group of people. In deciding whether an activity is a normal day-to-day activity, think about how far it is normal for a large number of people and whether it is carried out by people on a daily or frequent basis.

A normal day-to-day activity is not necessarily one that is carried out by a majority of people. For example, it's possible that some activities might be carried out only, or predominantly, by people of a particular gender. This includes activities such as applying make-up or using hair curling equipment. It can't be said to be normal for *most* people, but they would nevertheless be considered to be normal day-to-day activities.

Day-to-day activities are usually viewed in the widest sense of the phrase, and don't include activities that are confined to the day-to-day activities of a particular job. A day-to-day lifting activity might be lifting shopping, moving a chair, carrying a tray of food. It doesn't encompass the more demanding lifting tasks associated with some work places, for example, the sort of things that builders might be expected to lift on a construction site.

Example

Q had undergone open-heart surgery and was unable to lift heavy objects. He worked for B&Q at one of their garden centres. On the fifth day of his employment he was asked to assist in the handling of 200 litre peat sacks. He declined because of his heart condition and was dismissed on grounds of capability. He complained that he had been less favourably treated because of his disability. The tribunal found that he had a physical impairment but that this impairment did not affect his ability to carry out normal day-to-day activities, such as lifting shopping. Q was not therefore entitled to any reasonable adjustment to enable him to keep his job.

Quinlan v B&Q plc [1997]

Normal doesn't include specialised activities such as playing a musical instrument to a high standard of achievement, taking part in a particular game or hobby where very specific skills or level of ability are required, or playing a particular sport to a high level of ability, such as would be required for a professional footballer.

However, the decision in *Paterson v Commissioner of Police of the Metropolis (Metropolitan Police) [2007]* has shown that the courts interpret day-to-day activities very broadly.

In this case, P had reached a senior level in the police service before being diagnosed with dyslexia in 2004. He brought a complaint that he had been discriminated against because of his dyslexia in the course of a promotion examination. Although the police service was aware of his dyslexia and allowed him extra time to complete the exam, he still felt that he was placed at a disadvantage compared to other candidates. The employment tribunal accepted that the claimant needed 25% extra time to complete an assessment for promotion and that he was at a substantial disadvantage in comparison with non-dyslexic colleagues competing for superintendent positions. However the tribunal held that taking exams was not a normal day-to-day activity. P's dyslexia did not have more than a minor impact on his day-to-day activities and he was not disadvantaged when compared with the ordinary norm of the population as a whole.

On appeal the EAT reversed the decision, saying that employers should interpret 'normal day-to-day activities' widely and include activities which are relevant to participation in professional life and not just more mundane 'daily' tasks such as shopping. The judgement means that you should take a wider and more inclusive view of disabilities and not get caught up in technical arguments over the effect of the condition on the individual's abilities to carry out a limited range of day-to-day activities.

Where the disability is not obvious or the employer has no knowledge of it can the employer be liable? Authorities are mixed, but it seems the employer can be liable if the disability and worker's treatment are related.

Example

K was off work on sick leave for a lengthy period. The cause, diagnosis and prognosis were unclear. He attended an interview with the employer whose medical advisor had indicated that K was not fit to return to work. K told his employer he was due to see a specialist and asked him to wait the result of that meeting before deciding whether or not to dismiss. The employer refused and dismissed K next day. Shortly afterwards K was diagnosed with Chronic Fatigue Syndrome. The court decided K had been discriminated against even though the employer didn't know at the time that he had a disability.

H J Heinz Co Ltd v Kenrick [2000]

Note that you may be expected to know about a person's disability by putting together certain relevant facts. Ensure that where information about disabled employees may come though different channels there is a suitable and confidential process for collating and reviewing it. You can ask about disabilities as part of the recruitment process provided that you don't discriminate unjustifiably.

Example

H suffered from a psychiatric condition that could be controlled by medication, although she was not taking it. She applied for a position with the DWP. When she was interviewed, one member of the interview panel was someone who had known her for some time. She did not specifically disclose her condition to the DWP and declined to provide any information about her long-term condition in her health declaration form. She also refused permission for the DWP to contact her doctor.

Shortly after starting work H was involved in arguments with other members of staff, after which she was issued with an oral warning for misconduct. She was informed that disciplinary action would be taken if she failed to maintain the DWP's required standards of conduct. H subsequently applied for a disabled person's tax credit from the Inland Revenue and presented the application form to her manager who passed it on to DWP's HR department.

As a result of later incidents (both verbal and physical) between H and other members of staff, H was suspended and dismissed following a disciplinary hearing. The reason given for the dismissal was that she had failed to comply with departmental standards of behaviour because she repeatedly refused to comply with reasonable management requests and acted in a 'rude and threatening' manner. Her appeal against dismissal was rejected.

H complained successfully to an employment tribunal that she had suffered disability discrimination and that the DWP had failed to make reasonable adjustments. Her claim was upheld. The DWP argued that they did not have actual knowledge of her disability, but the court rejected the argument, saying that the employer had constructive knowledge of her psychiatric condition for a number of reasons.

- H's negative replies in the health declaration form and refused access to her GP or medical records, coupled with her volatile behaviour should have been a 'warning sign' to the DWP.

- A member of the interview panel knew H but did not mention anything about her health or disability.

- No further enquiries had been made following H's application for disability tax credit.

Department for Work and Pensions v Hall [2005]

Less Favourable Treatment

Discrimination arises where an employer, for a reason which relates to the disabled person's disability, unjustifiably treats that person less favourably than he treats or would treat others to whom the reason does not apply.

There are two questions to consider.

Firstly, was the individual treated less favourably for a reason which relates to his disability?

If so, did the employer treat him less favourably than he would treat others (or has treated others) to whom that reason does not apply?

Example

In the case of *London Borough of Lewisham v Malcolm [2008]*, the House of Lords overturned a longstanding legal principle. This judgement will have the effect of making it harder for employees to succeed in disability claims.

M suffered from schizophrenia. He was the tenant of a flat owned by LBC. The council sought a possession order after he sublet the flat without obtaining their consent. M claimed he would not have acted in such an irresponsible manner and sublet the flat had he not been schizophrenic. He alleged that in seeking to evict him, the council was discriminating against him by treating him less favourably for a reason that related to his disability.

The House of Lords dismissed M's claim. They accepted that, but for his disability, M would probably not have sublet the flat. However, they found that the reason the council was seeking possession of the flat was a housing management decision which had nothing to do with M's disability. Accordingly, and since disability must have played some part in the decision-making process for there to be disability-related discrimination, M's claim was bound to fail.

Despite the court's finding, a debate arose regarding the correct comparator for the purposes of disability-related discrimination. The majority of the Lords held that the correct analysis was to compare the way the disabled person has been treated to the way that a non-disabled person in the same situation would have been treated. In *Malcolm*, the correct comparator would have been a non-disabled tenant who had also illegally sublet.

In the case of the dismissal of a long-term absentee, the question would be whether the employer would have dismissed a non-disabled person who was also absent from work. This decision completely reverses the test established by the Court of Appeal in *Clark v Novacold [1999]*.

The Lords also held that an employer or service provider must know, or ought reasonably to know, about the disability before a finding of disability discrimination could be made. This also represents a significant change from earlier authorities.

An employer can dismiss a person who has a disability provided that he has exhausted the procedure and done all he can to make adjustments to help the employee remain in work.

Example

C had repeated long term absences from work owing to depression. His employers made every effort to accommodate him and to help him to return to work. C failed to co-operate with the employer's efforts to meet with him or even to comply with their attendance policies and procedures.

Eventually GCC dismissed him. C complained of discrimination, but the court found the employer's actions were justified.

Callaghan v Glasgow City Council [2001]

Once it has been established that the applicant has been treated less favourably for a reason related to his disability, a court would have to consider whether that less favourable treatment was justified.

An employer does not discriminate if he can show that the treatment was justified or that it did not relate to the disability. Less favourable treatment of a disabled person will be justified only if the reason for it is both material to the circumstances of the particular case and substantial. This means that the reason has to relate to the individual circumstances in question and not just be trivial or minor.

For example, someone who is blind and who is not short listed for a job involving computers because the employer thinks blind people cannot use them. If the employer makes no effort to look at the individual circumstances and simply makes a general assumption that blind people cannot use computers would not be able to justify his actions.

However, in the case of a person who has psoriasis and is rejected for a job involving modelling cosmetics on a part of the body which in his case is severely disfigured by the condition, the employer will be able to justify his decision. This would be lawful if the person's appearance would be incompatible with the purpose of the work. This is a substantial reason which is clearly related to the individual circumstances.

Less favourable treatment cannot be justified where the employer is under a duty to make a reasonable adjustment but fails to do so.

For example, an employee who uses a wheelchair is not promoted, solely because the work station for the higher post is inaccessible to wheelchairs, though it could readily be made so by rearrangement of the furniture. If the furniture had been re-arranged, the reason for refusing promotion would not have applied. The refusal of promotion would therefore not be justified.

Justification is not an easy test to satisfy. You will need to give careful thought as to whether it does actually apply and that there are sound business reasons for dismissing the employee which outweigh the detriment caused.

Reasonable Adjustments

As an employer, you are under a specific duty to make reasonable adjustments to accommodate the needs of a disabled employee. A reasonable adjustment is any step or steps that you can reasonably take to ensure that existing workplace arrangements don't put the disabled person at a disadvantage in comparison with a non-disabled person.

The duty applies where any physical feature of premises occupied by the employer, or any arrangements made by or on behalf of the employer, cause a substantial disadvantage to a disabled person compared with non-disabled people.

Some examples of possible adjustments are given below.

1. Making adjustments to premises. For example, an employer might have to make structural or other physical changes for wheelchair users, such as widening a doorway, providing a ramp or moving furniture.

2. Allocating duties to another person. Some duties might be reallocated to another employee if the disabled person has difficulty in doing them because of the disability. For example, if a job occasionally involves going onto the open roof of a building an employer might have to transfer this work away from an employee whose disability involves severe vertigo.

3. Transferring the person to fill an existing vacancy. If an employee becomes disabled, or has a disability which worsens so he cannot work in the same place or under

the same arrangements and there is no reasonable adjustment which would enable him to continue doing the current job, then he might have to be considered for any suitable alternative posts which are available. Such a case might also involve reasonable retraining.

4. Altering working hours. This could include allowing the disabled person to work flexible hours to enable additional breaks to overcome fatigue arising from the disability, or changing the disabled person's hours to fit with the availability of a carer.

5. Assigning the person to a different place of work. Consideration could be given to transferring a wheelchair user's work station from an inaccessible third floor office to an accessible one on the ground floor. It could mean moving the person to other premises of the same employer if the first building is inaccessible.

6. Allowing the person to be absent during working hours for rehabilitation, assessment or treatment. If a person were to become disabled, the employer might have to allow the person more time off during work than would be allowed to non-disabled employees, to receive physiotherapy, psychoanalysis or undertake employment rehabilitation.

7. Giving the person, or arranging for him to be given, training. This could be training in the use of particular pieces of equipment unique to the disabled person, or training appropriate for all employees but which needs altering for the disabled person because of the disability. For example, all employees might need to be trained in the use of a particular machine, but an employer might

have to provide slightly different or longer training for an employee with restricted hand or arm movements, or training in additional software for a visually impaired person so that he can use a computer with speech output.

8. Acquiring or modifying equipment. An employer might have to provide special equipment (such as an adapted keyboard for a visually impaired person or someone with arthritis), or an adapted telephone for someone with a hearing impairment or modified equipment (such as longer handles on a machine). There is no requirement to provide or modify equipment for personal purposes unconnected with work.

9. Modifying instructions or reference manuals. The way instruction is normally given to employees might need to be revised when telling a disabled person how to do a task. The format of instructions or manuals may need to be modified (e.g. produced in Braille or on audio tape) and instructions for people with learning disabilities may need to be conveyed orally with individual demonstration.

10. Modifying procedures for testing or assessment. Revise procedures to ensure that particular tests do not adversely affect people with particular types of disability. For example, a person with restricted manual dexterity might be disadvantaged by a written test, so an employer might have to give that person an oral test.

11. Providing a reader or interpreter. In some cases it might be appropriate to enlist a colleague to read mail to a person with a visual impairment at particular times

during the working day or, in certain circumstances, the hiring of a reader or sign language interpreter.

12. Providing supervision. This could involve the provision of a support worker, or help from a colleague, where appropriate, for someone whose disability leads to uncertainty or lack of confidence.

Generally cost will not be considered by the courts as sufficient good reason for failing to make an adjustment. Financial assistance can sometimes be made available. It's useful to talk to the DWP in the first instance for some guidance (www.dwp.gov.uk).

Where an existing employee becomes disabled, you are expected to make even greater efforts to make reasonable adjustments to keep him in employment.

Example

A was a road sweeper for Fife Council. After surgery she suffered complications and as a result was virtually unable to walk. She was accepted as disabled for the purposes of DDA.

She retrained and applied unsuccessfully for over 100 sedentary jobs. The council operated a competitive interviewing system (they appointed the best person for the job). Although A was qualified to do the job she was never the best candidate. Eventually she was dismissed on the grounds that she wasn't able to do her road sweeping job. Her disability discrimination claim was initially unsuccessful and eventually she appealed to the House of Lords.

The Lords allowed her appeal. The court held that the terms, conditions and arrangements relating to the essential functions of her employment were 'made by the employer' within the meaning of the DDA. As a result, A was disadvantaged compared with staff who were not disabled, as she was at risk of dismissal. Where an employee becomes incapable of performing the duties of his job the employer must make reasonable adjustments. In certain circumstances this could require an employer to transfer a disabled employee to an existing post at a slightly higher grade without requiring him to go through the competitive interviewing process.

A positive duty to make reasonable adjustments was therefore triggered. It may have been reasonable for the council to automatically transfer her to an existing post at a slightly higher grade, despite her not necessarily being the best person for the job.

This goes beyond what was previously considered a 'reasonable adjustment' under the DDA.

Archibald v Fife CC [2004]

In tackling the issue of reasonable adjustments, the starting point is to ask yourself what a disabled employee *can* do. If you start by thinking about what the employee can't do you're much more likely to reach the conclusion that he can't do anything. Remember, this legislation is designed to help those with disabilities continue working.

Dealing With Persistent Short-Term Absence

In order to manage sickness absences issues, it is important to fully understand the extent of the problem. There is a distinction to be made between short-term absences (where there is no underlying medical reason for the absence) and long-term absences. If there *is* an underlying reason for the absence, even though it manifests itself in short-term absences, (for example, an employee suffers from migraines), you should use the capability (often known as the long-term absence) route.

In some cases the employee may have a disability within the meaning of the DDA. This does place an extra duty on employers, but where you have exhausted all the options you can dismiss employees for disability-related absences. However, do exercise caution.

Example

D was employed as a staff nurse and often had to undertake one-to-one nursing of critically ill children. She had repeated sickness absences which caused severe operational difficulties for the Trust. The Trust's absence procedure had four stages. In D's case, stage one was triggered in June 2003. A stage two meeting was held in October 2003. A stage three meeting took place in January 2004 and this was followed by a stage four meeting in June 2004.

By June 2004, D had been closely monitored for a year. During that year she had lost 38% of her working time to sickness absence. She gave various reasons for that absence, including gynaecological problems, personal stress and stress caused by childcare difficulties.

At the stage four meeting, D contended, for the first time, that some of her absences in 2003 were due to migraines caused by drugs taken in connection with her gynaecological problems. She said that the problems would not recur because her medication had been changed. The Trust decided, however, to terminate her employment on the basis of her unacceptable absence levels.

D complained of disability discrimination. The tribunal assumed that D's gynaecological problems did amount to a disability and found that the Trust had discriminated against D on the ground of disability. It gave particular weight to two of D's absences which had related to migraines caused by the drugs taken for gynaecological problems. It found that had those absences been disregarded the stage two review would not have taken place. Therefore the stage four review should actually have been a stage three review and D would not have been at risk of dismissal in June 2004. It followed that her dismissal was for a reason that related to a disability.

The Trust appealed successfully. The EAT found that the tribunal had not properly considered whether D's treatment had been justified. It said that the DDA does not impose an absolute obligation on an employer to refrain from dismissing an employee who is absent wholly or partly on the grounds of ill-health due to a disability. It simply requires that such a dismissal is justified. A tribunal cannot conclude that a dismissal is not justified simply because the employee was absent on the ground of disability.

The EAT also disagreed with the tribunal's reasoning in discounting the stage two review. The EAT noted that the Trust's sickness absence procedure did not require it to disregard disability related absences. The EAT said that in deciding if the employer has acted unlawfully by taking such absences into account, the court will consider whether or not it is justified in doing so in the circumstances of a particular case. The EAT remitted the case to a fresh tribunal for a rehearing.

Royal Liverpool Children's NHS Trust v Dunsby [2006]

Any such approach should be cautious and you must be able to justify taking those absences into account when deciding to move along the stages of a sickness procedure, ultimately to dismissal.

Effective Strategies For Managing Short-Term Absence

The best way to manage short-term sickness absence is a combination of 'carrots and sticks'. Some examples of the sorts of things that employers can do to encourage good attendance are given below.

- Provide healthy food and life-style options at work (for example, fruit at meetings instead of biscuits, encouraging employees to have a break from the work place at lunchtime and perhaps go for a short walk).

- Hold RTW meetings on the employee's first day back.

- Where appropriate, hold informal welfare meetings.

- Take disciplinary procedures for unacceptable absence levels where this is no underlying medical reason for the absences.

- Use a trigger mechanism to review attendance and discuss with the employee as soon as it becomes a concern.

- Provide sickness absence information to line managers.

- Ensure line managers are trained to handle RTW and welfare meetings (and by the same token ensure they're carrying out their duties properly).

- Use your occupational health professionals effectively.

- Restrict sick pay.

Qualifying employees are entitled to receive Statutory Sick Pay (SSP), but often companies enhance that and pay some form of occupational sick pay (OSP). It is open to employers to attach conditions to the payment of OSP. Note that if you wish to restrict sick pay, then you must check that you are authorized to do so. If an employee qualifies for SSP and has fulfilled the requirements, then you must pay it.

Some examples of restrictions on OSP are non-payment in a case of:

- elective surgery; or

- sick notes submitted when an employee is taking time off under the emergency leave for dependents provisions; or

- sick notes submitted when the employee is undergoing or has just undergone formal disciplinary or grievance investigation or action; or

- sick notes submitted during a period of notice of termination of employment.

Note that even if you have a clause in your contract that allows you to withhold OSP if you are not satisfied as to the bona fide nature of the illness, you will still have to take medical advice in support of your argument.

Example

T worked for ME as a penalty fares inspector. Her shift ended at 11pm and she caught the last train home from Moorfields station. If this train wasn't running, she had to walk to James Street station in a different part of town. She didn't like doing this because she was scared of walking this distance late at night.

She raised her concerns with her manager who suggested that perhaps she should ask a colleague to accompany her to James Street. Alternatively she could wait for the Inspector later on, but this meant she would miss her train home.

On 20 May T asked her manager for assistance during the following week when she was rostered to work late. She knew Moorfields would be closed and she would have to walk to James Street.

Her manager said it was her responsibility to get herself to and from work. T left her shift on sick leave, which lasted seven weeks.

She had GP sick notes covering her sick leave period but she was told that she would not be paid OSP because her employer didn't accept that she was genuinely ill. She complained successfully to the tribunal that ME had unlawfully deducted her pay.

The doctor's certificates were clear as to the reason for absence. ME had ignored the medical certificates and had not undertaken any medical investigation of its own that might have put in doubt the opinion of the GP.

The court said that even if she had originally been feeling piqued at not getting her way, then so long as that had led to the genuine stress condition that caused her absence, she was entitled to OSP in the absence of contradictory medical evidence.

Merseyrail Electrics 2002 Ltd v Taylor [2007]

Disciplinary Action

Disciplinary procedures for unacceptable absence may be used to make it clear to employees that you won't tolerate unjustified absence and that you will enforce your absence policies. If you take disciplinary action, there must be a clear standard of attendance for the business and you have to be able to show evidence that the employee is below that standard.

Where an employee's absence has exceeded your trigger point, the first step is to talk to him about it. Tell him that his absence is causing problems. Investigate the matter thoroughly. Try to find out whether the absences are due to genuine illnesses. Don't make assumptions about the causes of the absence.

Speak privately to the employee, informally in the first instance. Set a time limit for an improvement in his performance. Tell him clearly and specifically what improvement you require and what will happen if that improvement is not achieved. Make a record of the discussion.

An employee may accuse you of picking on him because he is sick. However, your concern is with his low attendance levels rather than his sickness.

You may want to consider taking medical advice to establish whether there is an underlying medical condition. If there is no underlying medical reason for the absences, continue to treat this through the disciplinary route as a matter of poor attendance.

If there is an underlying medical reason for the absences, use the long-term absence procedure (see page 82).

If, after an informal discussion, the employee's attendance has not improved to the required standard within the specified time frame, you can move matters forward to a first stage formal warning. At this point the absence problem is often treated as a form of misconduct and will be dealt with according to the company's disciplinary procedure.

You can issue formal warnings related to poor attendance. The expected standard of attendance – in other words, the target – must be very clear. Your employee must be given a reasonable period of time to demonstrate whether he can achieve the specified attendance standard.

If, at the end of the warning period, the employee's attendance has still not reached the required level, continue following your disciplinary procedure. Ultimately this will lead to dismissal.

It is fair to terminate employment for poor attendance, even where the employee has produced a medical certificate for his absences. The dismissal is for a failure to reach a reasonable level of attendance, not about whether the individual was genuinely ill or not. Dismissal in this case will be for some other substantial reason (SOSR) i.e. poor attendance.

Example

T was employed as a racquet stringer. Her record for the first two years of her employment was satisfactory. Thereafter her attendance record became increasingly poor. For the last 18 months of her employment she was absent on average for about 25 per cent of her working time. Nearly all of these absences were covered by medical certificate. These referred to conditions such as 'dizzy spells', 'anxiety and nerves', 'bronchitis', 'viral infections' and 'flatulence'. She received a number of warnings about her persistent absence. These warnings set her targets for improvement and clearly indicated the consequences of failure to improve.

The company consulted their own medical advisor. He could see no common link between the illnesses and said that T was not suffering from any long-term illness. When T returned to work she was summoned to a meeting and later that day she was dismissed. She claimed unfair dismissal. The tribunal found that she had been fairly dismissed because she had been clearly advised of the required attendance levels and the consequences of breach.

International Sports Co v Thomson [1980]

This is an old case. These days you should ask an employee like T to see your Occupational Medical Advisor (OMA), rather than rely on an assessment of her sick notes. You should also remember to write, setting up the disciplinary meeting, offer the right to be accompanied and give some reasonable time for the employee to prepare.

Long-Term Sickness Absence

Managing long-term sickness absence, or short term absence where there is an underlying medical reason for the absences is a very different process. Long-term absence is nearly always the result of physical or mental ill health. In many organizations there will be pressure to replace the employee, which must be handled cautiously. There are several questions to ask.

- Just how much damage is being caused by this absence?

- How long will the absence continue for?

- What is the prognosis of the employee's general practitioner or the organization's doctor?

- Will there be a full recovery or would a return to the same work be imprudent?

- Is alternative work available, with re-training if necessary?

- How long has the employee been working for the organization?

- Have all possibilities been discussed with the employee and his representative?

You can fairly dismiss an employee who has long-term health problems, even if he is suffering from a disability. Under the DDA you must take all reasonable steps to adjust the work and the workplace in order to accommodate the disability. Once you have exhausted the possibilities, you do not have to continue to employ a disabled employee who can no longer carry out the job. Note that where an employee becomes disabled while in your employment, you are under an extra duty to make reasonable adjustments.

If the time eventually arrives when all procedures have been exhausted, all avenues explored and the job can no longer be kept open, the employee should be fully consulted and informed about possible dismissal. In reaching a decision to dismiss you must ensure that capability or dismissal procedures have been correctly followed.

Dismissal by reason of capability (including medical incapability), is a potentially fair reason for dismissal. Failure to identify the correct reason for dismissal can contribute to a finding of unfair dismissal. Having identified the reason for dismissal, a tribunal will consider if the appropriate procedures have been followed.

It is also important that you act fairly in treating the illness as the reason for dismissal. Your action must always be within the band of reasonable responses. There are a number of factors a tribunal may consider relevant.

- The nature and length of any illness or disability.

- Past service and record.

- Any demonstrable improvement in the attendance record.

- The effect of continued absence on colleagues and the effect of the absence on the employer's services. Can cover be easily arranged? Tribunals must consider the size and administrative resources of the business when assessing whether the actions were reasonable.

- Whether there are there any offers of alternative employment. This perhaps has more relevance in relation to long-term sick employees, but will be relevant in the context of an employee who may have a disability. The Disability Discrimination Act 1995 requires an employer to make reasonable adjustments and this can mean looking at alternative employment.

The law does not provide specific time periods for waiting for a sick employee to return to work. The key here is to involve and consult the employee at all stages.

Keeping in contact is a key factor in helping employees return to work after a long-term absence. Without reasonable contact those who are absent may feel out of touch and undervalued

Make sure your conversation with the absent employee is clearly focused on his well-being and return to work. Try to focus as much on what he can do as well as things he may need help with.

If the employee 'goes to earth' and won't talk to you, leave him a little space, but do open up efforts to talk again. If the employee still won't talk to you after a reasonable period of time, arrange for another manager to speak with him. Be flexible and offer to visit the employee's home, provide assistance to enable him to attend the meeting or to meet in a neutral place. Take medical advice to try to discover the reasons for the difficulty.

The employee is under a duty to carry out a reasonable management request and that would include meeting for a welfare conversation or to attend a formal capability meeting, unless there are substantial reasons for not doing so.

For examples of letters encouraging a reluctant employee to talk see Appendix 3.

If the employee has suffered a traumatic injury or sudden illness, extend your sympathies and use discretion until the longer prognosis is known.

In the case of planned treatment, employees may welcome hospital visits but try to check with relatives first.

If you are notified that an employee is suffering from a stress-related illness, make contact within a week. Note that it is unlikely he will be ready to discuss returning at this stage. Use discretion until the longer-term prognosis is known.

Checklist

- Take time to know your employees and the things that affect their health, as this will help you to decide the kind of contact they would welcome while sick.

- Create a climate of trust by agreeing methods, frequency and reasons for keeping in contact with absent employees.

- Where appropriate consider a phased return to work over where the time spent at work increases over a period of weeks. This can be especially useful where an employee is suffering from low-level stress and anxiety conditions or where he has been absent from the workplace for some time.

- Consult employees, HR managers and trade union representatives, who may be well placed to offer advice on how to make return to work more easy, although be careful not to discuss an employee's medical condition without their knowledge and consent.

- Be flexible. Treat each case individually, but on a fair and consistent basis.

- If the employee is able to travel, suggest he comes in to see colleagues at lunch time or coffee breaks.

- Welcome the employee back to work after absence and carry out RTW interviews.

- Give employees the opportunity to discuss their health or other concerns in private.

- Take professional advice, where necessary.

- Remember that medication can have side effects on things such as physical stamina, mood, driving, machinery operation and safety-critical tasks.

Just as there are some things to ensure you do, there are also some things to ensure you avoid doing. Don't:

- just leave a sick employee for months with no contact;

- wait until someone goes on long-term absence to consider the best way for you to manage sickness absence (instead, plan ahead in partnership with your management team, trade union and employee representatives);

- put off making contact or pass responsibility to someone else unless there are sound reasons for doing so;

- make assumptions about the employee's situation or their medical circumstances;

- discuss the employee's circumstances without that person's knowledge and consent;

- put pressure on employees to discuss their return to work before they are ready;

- say that colleagues are under pressure or that work is piling up.

Remember that recovery times for the same condition can vary significantly from person to person.

Dismissal For Capability

As with short-term absence, you should follow a clearly-established procedure.

Step 1: set a time limit

Tell your employee that there is a time limit on holding the job open for his return to work. Discuss the employee's current state of health and the likelihood of a return to work within a reasonable period with him. Also discuss what alternative work he may be able to do.

Ask for the employee's permission to talk to his doctor, and arrange to obtain a medical opinion. If the doctor is unwilling or unable to give an opinion as to when the employee will be able to return to work, ask for him to be examined by a third party.

Your rules should indicate a general time limit for sickness absence, after which you will take action. Make sure you tell your employee clearly what your time limit is. Consider taking action when sick pay is about to expire.

Step 2: investigate other options

What can we do to help the employee return to work? These could include:

- adjustments to the workplace;

- a different work location;

- a change or reduction of hours;

- equipment to help him do the job;

- re-training;

- light or limited duties.

Keeping full records of these conversations is essential. These should include details of your discussions about the options available and your efforts to find solutions.

When you have the medical opinion and it is still clear that the employee is unlikely to be able to return to work, discuss the steps the company proposes to take with him.

If the employee is not likely to return, serve proper notice of termination of employment.

Step 3: dismissal

If you have reached your deadline and the employee is unable to return or cope with alternative employment options in the foreseeable future, issue his dismissal notice, taking care to state the reason for dismissal is on the grounds of capability. Offer the right of appeal against dismissal.

Example

D had been employed by the Local Authority since 1959. He was dismissed from his position as Principal Assistant Surveyor. He was aged 56. He had had a history of ill health and at the time of his dismissal had been off sick for five full months.

The employer wrote to the District Community Physician and asked him to indicate whether D's ill health was such that he should be retired on the grounds of ill health. The District Community Physician asked another doctor to examine the employee and produce reports. On the basis of this report from a second physician, the District Community Physician wrote to the company stating that the employee was unfit and should be dismissed. The employers then wrote to the employee and dismissed him.

There was no real consultation or effort to make adjustments for D. The letter to the District Community Physician asked a question which should be decided by management. Doctors only provide medical information about his medical condition and the likelihood of his return to work.

The dismissal was for a fair reason but it was procedurally unfair and therefore D had been unfairly dismissed.

East Lindsay Council v Daubney [1977]

Occasionally an employee whose employment ends because of his sickness or injury may return to work. This is very rare, but note that the employee's continuity of employment may be preserved for up to 26 weeks if he can show that he was incapable of work as a result of his sickness or injury. The key point here is the link between the two periods of employment and whether the main cause of the absence was the employee's incapacity.

The Doctor Dilemma – Getting Medical Advice

If the absences are for a series of apparently unrelated reasons, you are not legally required to take up medical evidence, although it would be a sensible idea to do so before moving on to disciplinary action. The courts would expect you to take medical advice before moving to dismiss an employee.

A report may indicate that there is an underlying genuine medical condition, which did not originally appear to be the case. There have been some cases where the doctor's report has confirmed that the absentee has not been to the doctor's surgery for some considerable time, indicating that the absences are not all genuine.

Employers have to try to understand the nature of an illness, the prognosis and what they can do to support the employee, but getting useful medical advice is notoriously difficult.   There are a number of reasons for this.

- Extreme vagueness resulting in a lack of precise information.

- Answering a question other than the one asked or missing out some replies.

- Use of such dense medical jargon that the employer is no wiser than when he started.

- A tendency to travel far beyond what is required in terms of medical information and to give advice or opinion on other, unrelated matters.

- Slow (or no) response.

If you get a report including these sorts of replies it can be expensive and frustrating. In terms of getting the best advice it's probably best to 'grow your own' medical information resources by forming a relationship with an OMA. That way the OMA will start to know something about your organization and about your management style. As he does so he will give better quality information. You may still have to provide some guidance, but at least you can get the relevant information. For example, one employee had been absent for three months and was refusing to attend a welfare meeting. We asked the OMA to see her and included the following paragraph in the letter accompanying the medical questionnaire:

Because she has been away for three months now, we have asked Susie to attend a welfare meeting. She has refused to see us. We don't understand why this has become an issue. Certainly, nothing in our conversations so far has really explained it. We have assured her that she has nothing to fear. We simply want to understand through an informal conversation how matters stand and to work with her to promote her recovery.

Carrying out a welfare meeting with an employee who has been unwell for some time is purely standard practice. We need to make sure she's well enough to attend this meeting and would welcome your advice on this point.

We got the answer we needed and Susie duly attended the welfare meeting.

See Appendix 4 for a sample letter to doctor and an accompanying medical questionnaire.

Occupational Health Advisor V Employee's Own GP

There will always be a role for the employee's own GP (or other medical advisor). Quite often they are very protective of their patient and give very little useful information. The most effective way of tackling this is to use a style of short questions, each one asking for fairly minimal information. Rather than asking 'what's wrong with Joe Bloggs' I ask "Joe Bloggs says that he has XYZ. Please confirm that this is the case." This is completely at odds with my usual open question style, but it seems to work.

If you propose to contact the employee's own GP or a medical advisor who has been treating him, you will need written permission from the employee to do so. These days most companies have an express term in their contracts requiring an employee to see an OMA or other medical advisor of the company's choice. Where this is the case you can require the employee to attend the meeting otherwise he will be in breach of contract.

If there is no such term in your contract you cannot require him to attend.

Occasionally, an employee who has been absent for apparent sickness refuses to give permission for you to write to his medical advisor. If this is the case explain to him that you need to get the best information you can to help decide about the next steps. Give him a little time to review his original opinion. However, if he continues to refuse, you will note his refusal and make a decision based on the facts available to you.

Access to Medical Reports Act 1988

Where a medical report is prepared by the employee's own GP (or other medical advisor) this legislation allows a person to see the report before it comes to the company. The employee has the right to state that he wishes to see the report. Additionally he can withhold consent to the report being supplied to the employer or request amendments to the report.

Where the employee states that he wishes to have access to the report, you must let the GP know this when making the application and at the same time let the employee know that the report has been requested.

The employee doesn't have the right to see the report if it has been prepared by a specialist or company doctor who has not had any responsibility for the medical care of the employee.

Conflicting Medical Reports

It's fairly common in ill-health cases for there to be conflicting advice on the prognosis for an employee's return to work. You can prefer one doctor's opinion over another, as long as you have reasonable grounds to explain your choice

Example

In *Heathrow Express Operating Company Limited v Jenkins*, the EAT provided useful guidance on how employers should deal with conflicting medical evidence in disability discrimination cases and on the employer's duty to make reasonable adjustments.

J was employed by HE as a customer services representative. Her main duties were to ensure that trains arrived and departed safely. A number of these tasks were categorised as 'safety-critical' and 'safety-related' work. Under the Railways (Safety Critical Work) Regulations 1996, employers must ensure that employees who undertake such work are fit and competent to do so. Failure to comply is a criminal offence.

In 2002, J was involved in a distressing incident at work and sustained a personal injury, leading to a long period of sickness absence. She tried to return to work but began to suffer from panic attacks, a condition which meant that she was classified as disabled for the purposes of the DDA. Throughout her period of absence, the company took medical advice on J's fitness to return to work and sought to discover what adjustments they could make to assist that return and whether she was fit and competent to be engaged in safety-related and safety-critical work.

Eventually, the company had advice from three different medical professionals. One consultant psychiatrist felt that J would make a recovery and that she could eventually resume her normal role. Another consultant psychiatrist considered that she had excellent prospects of making a full recovery without any permanent incapacity and suggested that a return to work programme should be instigated as soon as possible.

Dr Bell, the company's occupational health physician disagreed with both reports. His advice was that although J was well enough to return to work in a general sense, she should be permanently restricted from undertaking safety-critical activities. He also suggested that Heathrow should examine closely whether or not she was suitable for safety-related activities.

The company considered that Dr Bell's report was crucial. In particular, they relied on his view that no reasonable adjustments could be made allow J to continue in her 'safety-critical' role. A number of attempts were made to find her alternative work, but none could be found and she was dismissed in January 2006.

J complained of disability-related discrimination, a failure to make reasonable adjustments and unfair dismissal.

In the EAT the court held that the company were entitled to rely on the report of the occupational health physician and to conclude that there were no reasonable adjustments that could be made to allow J to do safety critical work. Faced with conflicting medical evidence, the company was entitled to rely on Dr Bell's status as an occupational health physician and to prefer his advice, as long as they did not act irrationally or perversely in favouring his opinion over those given by other medical professionals. As a result, they were entitled to have concluded that there were no reasonable adjustments that would allow J to return to work. This, coupled with the fact that they had a substantive reason for dismissing and that the correct dismissal procedures had been followed, meant that the dismissal was fair.

Workplace Stress

Pundits estimate that depression causes an estimated £23.1 billion per year in lost output to the economy and that nearly 13 million working days are lost each year due to work-related stress, anxiety or depression.

The Health and Safety Executive (HSE) defines stress as:

'The adverse reaction people have to excessive pressure or other types of demand placed on them. It arises when they worry that they cannot cope.'

The word 'stress' has been used to describe a variety of states, ranging from mild anxiety to serious psychiatric illness. It's important to remember that stress itself is not an illness, but it can be a cause and/or be a symptom of a number of serious illnesses, so you should not ignore such complaints. Different people respond in varying degrees to different stimuli and experience very different levels of stress. Most people hate – *really* hate – the idea of public speaking. Not me! I'm like Rumpole, never happier than when hoisting myself on to the old hind legs to have a nice chat with a receptive audience about employment law, wonderful, exciting subject that it is. (I should get out more, shouldn't I?). Some people like bungy-jumping. They do it for fun, I'm told. I cannot bear heights and simply couldn't jump off some building or mountain for fun or any other reason. Even the idea of doing so makes me feel slightly sick and dizzy.

So the point is that one size doesn't fit all. It might be tempting to dismiss as an over-reaction an employee's complaints of stress if you don't experience the same reaction in the same circumstances. The fact is that the employee may well experience a different and greater response from the one you might have, however unreasonable you think it is, and it is *that* response you have to deal with.

There are a number of risks to an employer of not dealing with workplace stress.

- Breach of the health and safety legislation.

- Constructive unfair dismissal claims .

- Disability discrimination claims.

- Personal injury claims.

Example

H was a Licensed House Manager at an SCR pub in Luton. He refused to opt out of the Working Time Regulations (WTR) and so had not agreed to work more than 48 hours per week on average. His records showed that over a two-month period he worked between 89 and 92 hours a week. He complained to his employer that he was working excessively long hours and that he felt tired. They agreed that an assistant manager should be appointed, but had done nothing about this before H collapsed and sued the company for negligence.

H had not suffered previous mental illness and had not informed anyone that his health was being affected by the stress of work. However, because he had complained about his workload before his collapse and the provisions of the WTR had been ignored by the company, the court decided that it was reasonably foreseeable that he would suffer a psychiatric injury.

Six Continents Retail Ltd v Hone [2005]

Historically, it has been very difficult for an employee to claim damages for psychiatric injury against his employer, as it was necessary to show that such psychiatric injury was reasonably foreseeable.

There is a common law duty in every contract of employment that the employer will take care of employees' health and safety. The first case in which an employee successfully claimed against his employer was *Walker v Northumberland County Council [1995]*, in which the employer was held to be liable for psychiatric injury caused to a social services employee through stress. The case determined that employers may be in breach of their duty of care towards employees if they place them under such a degree of work pressure as to damage their health. The facts in *Walker* were as follows.

Example

W was employed as a social worker dealing with cases of child abuse. His workload had steadily increased over a number of years and in 1986 he had a nervous breakdown. The following year he had recovered sufficiently to return to work and he was promised additional resources to help him with his workload. Despite these assurances, the support failed to materialise and he had a second breakdown six months later. W sued the council, arguing that they were in breach of their duty of care to provide a safe working environment.

The court found that the council could not be held liable for W's first breakdown. The employer could not have reasonably foreseen that W was exposed to a significant risk of mental illness through his job.

However, in relation to the second nervous breakdown, the court held that the council could have reasonably foreseen that such an outcome was a real risk, given that the kind of workload and work pressures which led to the first breakdown had persisted. The council was in breach of its duty of care by failing to provide effective support to alleviate W's workload.

In this case the employee succeeded in his claim because he was able to establish four factors.

1. That the employer had breached their duty of care towards him by being negligent.

2. That he had suffered a clinical psychiatric injury or illness.

3. That the injury to health was caused by stress at work.

4. That the injury to his health was reasonably foreseeable.

As a result of this case, employers should be aware that they need to be mindful of the possibilities of employees suffering damage to their mental health as a result of workplace pressures, such as an overload of work. In particular, where an employee has complained about an excessive workload, of work-related stress or of unreasonable demands being placed upon him at work, then the employer should take action to alleviate the problems. Where a valid complaint has been made and the employer has failed to take appropriate remedial action and where the employee's health suffers, this could be classed as a breach of the duty to take care, entitling the employee to claim damages.

In 2002, the Court of Appeal considered the question of occupational stress claims in a number of cases. They made it clear that the same principles apply to stress claims as to ordinary industrial accidents. In other words, it is necessary to show that the kind of harm suffered by the particular employee was reasonably foreseeable.

Although the Court of Appeal in Sutherland (Chairman of the Governors of St Thomas Becket RC High School) v Hatton [2002] suggested that employers are entitled to rely on what the employee tells them, they are nevertheless expected to investigate where they believe something is wrong. One of the cases heard at the same time as Hatton went on appeal to the House of Lords. The Lords' decision made it clear that employers can't just ignore signs of distress, even where the employee is not altogether clear about the state of his health.

Example

B was head of the maths department at East Bridgwater Community School. Following a restructuring in 1995 all of the teachers at his level were being overworked. B found the changes and increased hours very stressful.

Despite raising concerns with his employer, he received little sympathy, and soon became ill with stress and depression. He did not tell anyone about his symptoms before taking three weeks off work in May 1996. When he returned to work, he said that he was finding things difficult. His symptoms continued and when he returned in the autumn term, the head teacher asked a colleague to keep an eye on him. In November 1996 B suffered a nervous breakdown and was advised to stop work immediately.

B sued his employer for damages for personal injury, and was awarded more than £100,000. This decision was overturned by the Court of Appeal and B appealed to the House of Lords.

Their Lordships found that after his first sickness absence, his employer should at least have made sympathetic enquiries and considered what could have been done to help. While employers can assume that employees are up to their job (unless otherwise indicated) a duty may arise if any steps can be taken to assist an employee who is having difficulty coping. B's employer was found wanting and as such had breached its duty of care and was liable in negligence.

Barber v Somerset County Council [2004]

Foreseeability depends upon what the employer knows (or ought reasonably to know) about the individual employee. It is not enough for the employee to show that occupational stress has caused the harm. He must show that a breach of duty committed by the employer caused, or materially contributed to, the harm suffered.

The key points from the Court of Appeal judgement 2002 are shown in Appendix 5.

Although there is no legislation specifically covering stress, employers have a responsibility to identify and reduce or remove stressful factors in the workplace. There is a general duty of care under health and safety legislation. Employers have a duty to carry out a health and safety risk assessment. The duty includes identifying risks to mental health as well as physical health. This means that you should take whatever steps you reasonably can to reduce or remove the risks. If you fail to do so and that failure results in an employee suffering a reasonably foreseeable injury, you are likely to be required to pay compensation to the employee for loss that they may suffer as a result of the injury. There is no cap on the compensation that can be awarded.

In addition, you have an obligation under the Health and Safety at Work Act to take reasonably practicable measures to ensure the health, safety and welfare of your employees. A failure to do so can result in a criminal conviction and a fine and/or imprisonment. More specifically, the WTR also impose limits on average weekly working hours and require you to give employees daily and weekly rest breaks and paid holidays.

Reducing The Risk Of Stress

You can do a number of things to help to reduce stress in the workplace. Think through all the factors which can create stressful working conditions, such as the work environment, organizational culture and management style, job design, organizational structures and personal issues, and take preventative action where possible.

Some possible measures to reduce stress are listed below.

1. Conduct an assessment of stress hazards in the workplace to measure stress and its causes. Carry out a risk assessment to identify the risks to the health and safety of any person arising out of, or in connection with work, or the conduct of the undertaking. This includes risks to both physical and mental health. While most people respond well to a certain level of pressure, be aware of the personal and organizational signs that an individual may be under more pressure at work than he can cope with. There may be warning signs of increased stress levels from employees, such as higher-than-usual numbers of sickness absences or changes in usual patterns of behaviour.

2. Consider having a stress policy containing organizational commitments to minimise any potential work-related stress claims. Such a policy would set out guidance to both employees and managers on how to effectively identify and manage stress in the workplace.

3. Introduce training on stress awareness, coping skills and managing stress.

4. Set out the responsibilities of all the parties.

5. If possible, you should make available a confidential counselling service for employees and bring it to their attention, for example, by referring to it in staff handbooks and by advertising it on notice boards, websites and newsletters.

6. Review employment practices and job specifications to assess whether it is really necessary for employees to work long hours. Regard should be paid to the requirements of the WTR.

7. When appointing a person to a job that may be stressful, emphasise the stressful nature of the work and ask him to consider carefully whether he can cope with such demands.

8. If it is likely that employees will work long hours, consider asking them to sign the opt-out from the 48-hour week. Note that an employee must not suffer detriment for refusing to opt out. Keep an eye on them to ascertain whether they are coping with the hours.

9. Ensure that employees have a reasonably managed workload and that management systems are in place to give employees the kind of support they require to carry out tasks satisfactorily.

10. Explore employees' concerns fully if they are raised with you.

Where an employee actually tells you that he's not coping, it may be hard for you to evade liability for any subsequent breakdown unless reasonable steps had been taken to reduce the burden on the employee.

The Court of Appeal's advice in Hatton suggests that employers can take what employees say at face value. But don't take that too literally. Employers have to be proactive in dealing with problems. Offering a counselling service in isolation is not enough to discharge your responsibilities.

Example

D was employed as a finance assistant by Intel from September 1988 until June 2001. She made numerous complaints about pressure of work. There was a major management re-organization in October 2000, which resulted in a new Employee Services Group. D applied for and became Mergers and Acquisitions Payroll Integration Analyst. This resulted in increased responsibilities, excessive working hours and further pressure of work.

D had a history of resolved post-natal depression, requiring time off work after the birth of each of her two children in October 1995 and March 1998. D brought a personal injury claim, issuing proceedings against her employer for damages for personal injury arising from the employer's negligence, breach of statutory duty, and duty of care.

The initial trial judge held that D's work was rated as outstanding by her employer, but her reporting lines were confused, and prioritising the demands made upon her by different managers was problematic. Although D had complained about her workload in e-mails, and was found in tears by one of her line managers, no urgent action plan was put in place immediately to reduce her workload.

The company denied liability on the grounds that she hadn't used the counselling service. The court found that the counselling service could be of little or no help to D. It could not reduce her workload. The company was found liable, as D's injuries were foreseeable in the circumstances.

On appeal the Court of Appeal agreed that an employer's short-term counselling service could not have reduced the risk of a breakdown, since it did not reduce her workload (the cause of the stress). At most, the service could only have advised D to see her own doctor and was insufficient to discharge the employer's duty to provide a safe working environment.

The court accepted that the employer did not have prior knowledge that the employee was susceptible to work-related depression. Despite this lack of knowledge, the employer was still held liable, because it was aware of D's excessive workload.

Daw v Intel Corporation [2007]

The decision in *Daw* tells us that where an employee is experiencing stress relating to excessive workloads, having a workplace counselling service will not in itself discharge your duty of care in stress claims. Even if you have systems in place to support staff who are suffering from work-related stress, this is no substitute for putting an action plan in place to reduce their workload. Failure to do so will result in a finding of negligence.

If an employee does complain that work-related stress has caused him an illness or injury, investigate the causes and symptoms with the employee and take steps to understand the medical issues. Try to establish what has caused the condition and if it is a work-related issue what you need to do in order to address the cause. Find out what the employee is doing to address the matter and what you can do to help.

Where appropriate, it can be helpful to agree with an employee a plan for him to return to work in a limited capacity, increasing over several weeks. People are sociable animals and being at home with nothing but daytime TV for company can impede recovery. Including him in the social context of the work environment reduces the sense of isolation and increases the chances of an early return to work.

All of this should happen before you take any steps against the employee concerned in relation to their absence.

If absence from work for stress is likely to lead to dismissal, you must ensure that you have proper medical evidence of the employee's state of health and explore the possibility of a return to work with the employee.

Employers are under a duty to carry out an assessment of risks at work, both physical and mental and do what they can to reduce or remove those risks. The assessment should identify what the risks are, how they arise and how they impact on those affected. This information is needed so that the decisions on how to manage those risks are made in an informed, rational and structured manner and the action taken is proportionate.

The HSE has produced a number of publications to help employers deal with the management of stress at work, including a set of 'Management Standards' to help employers comply with their legal obligations and to prioritise and measure performance in managing work related stress.

- Look for hazards.

- Decide who might be harmed and how.

- Evaluate the risks and decide whether the existing precautions are adequate or whether more should be done.

- Record your findings.

- Review your assessment from time to time and revise if necessary.

Handling Stress At Work

From the work that I've done with clients in recent years I'm left with the clear impression that the use of 'stress' to describe a condition is being very over-worked. Considering that stress isn't even an illness, but a necessary part of being alive, it has become something of a problem for managers. In seeking to support their patients (and with the best of intentions) doctors can sometimes cloud the issues by providing sick notes which say things like 'stress', 'fatigue' or 'general debility'. I've even seen sick notes that say 'family problems' and 'bereavement'. None of this is helpful in trying to address the employee's difficulties.

In these circumstances employers are rather left holding the baby and you have to be rigorous about investigating the matter with the employee and trying to do whatever you reasonably can to support him in his recovery.

There seem to be a number of categories. Some employees will become genuinely ill with a psychiatric illness. It may be triggered by all sorts of things, such as events affecting friends or family death or illness or something that's built up over a period of time outside work. It could be work related issues. Sometimes it's a combination of things and the employee simply feels overwhelmed.

Some employees may work very hard for a while, become tired and take a day or two off sick with stress as a means to recovery (this often happens with shift work and where people are paid overtime for doing extra work).

There are undoubtedly employees who take convenient refuge in having stress when they hear something they don't want to hear or are asked to do something they don't want to do, or else are being taken through the disciplinary process.

Example

A senior manager, D, was found to have been accessing and downloading vast amounts of pornographic material during, before and after working hours. This was in breach of the company's internet procedures and considered to be a matter of gross misconduct. During the initial meeting to investigate the alleged breach, D admitted to breaching the rules.

He was subsequently suspended to allow the investigation to be completed. He tried several times to persuade the company to allow him to resign on favourable terms, but it refused to do so. D then went to his doctor and was signed off sick with depression. The manager dealing with the matter, S, expressed concern for D (and indeed the company provided some financial help so that he could see a psychiatric consultant), but advised that the investigation would continue and it would contact D in writing with the outcome.

D appointed a legal advisor who also sought to agree favourable terms for a resignation. The company said that it was open to D to resign but that it would continue with the investigation. Once the investigation was concluded S wrote to D setting up a formal disciplinary hearing. S also advised him that once the company had entered into the formal process then it would not accept a resignation. This had the effect of producing a resignation thirty minutes before the hearing, which the company accepted.

As employers we do have a duty to deal appropriately with these various situations. Our responses will vary depending on the circumstances

Where an employee is seriously ill, for example he's had a nervous breakdown, we have to work with the medical advisor to understand the nature of the problem and to plan if and how the employee may be able to return to work. This is likely to be a long-term plan and you should keep in regular touch with the employee and his medical advisor.

If we notice that an employee works hard most of the time, including doing a lot of overtime for six or seven weeks at a stretch then goes off for a few days with stress, take a different approach. It could be that the employee gets tired, or simply thinks "I've done my bit for the last few weeks. It's time to have a break". We'll investigate and try to find out the stress symptoms, what the employee thinks is prompting the condition and what he thinks we can do to help him break the cycle. Always remind the employee that we'll do what we reasonably can to help him return to work and ask for his thoughts on how to improve matters so that he's able to cope without having to take the time off every six weeks. Note all this down. Have your kit bag of ideas and suggestions ready (yoga, meditation tapes, etc) so that if he says, "Well, I'm having trouble sleeping" you can ask him what he's doing about the problem and be able to offer some ideas as an alternative to getting sleeping pills from the doctor. Monitor progress and review with him.

There are some people who use stress as a way of evading responsibility and/or as a way of attacking their manager. Let's just remind ourselves that while there are employees like this, the vast majority are good, hard-working people who want to do a good job. Always take the approach that the employee is a genuine case, even when your baser nature suggests that it is not.

Example

A couple of years ago I was asked to get involved with helping a young man, P, who had allegedly been help up at knife point. Since the incident he had been off work with stress. If P had indeed been held up at knife point (and it was indeed a possibility) I can imagine that it would be extremely stressful. The problem was that P had such a poor attendance record that everyone thought he was 'crying wolf'. Only P really knows.

By the time I saw P he had been away from work for six weeks. The sixth to eighth week of absence is often quite a critical time in attendance management, because it's round that time that employees get used to being at home and out of the way of the work routine. It's therefore rather more difficult to get them to focus on coming back to work. I asked P to talk me through his symptoms to help me understand the difficulties he was experiencing and then asked what was happening about addressing them.

P told me he was having problems sleeping and that he was seeing a counsellor. Further questioning revealed that he hadn't started seeing the counsellor and had not yet made a date to do so. I asked him for the counsellor's name and address and when he proposed to start the therapy. I also asked for permission to write to the counsellor once the therapy was part-way through to investigate how well P was responding.

Then I asked what else he was doing to help himself recover. "I have the love and support of my family," P answered.

By this time I was in full 'headmistress' flow and said that I thought that the support of his family was no doubt invaluable, but he would probably need rather more specialist help in the short or medium term. Again I asked him what he was doing to help himself. The discussion was steered towards yoga and meditation and P, slightly bemused by the turn the conversation had taken, agreed to try some yoga. This commitment was noted down and then we talked about a phased return to work. Being herd animals, most of us don't really thrive at home alone for any length of time and in fact it can actually make us feel depressed. Remember, in years gone by solitary confinement was one of the worst punishments inflicted on prisoners.

I suggested that we try a slow phased return, so that P could come in for a couple of hours the following week and see how he got on. We would monitor the plan carefully and adjust it to meet his requirements. P agreed and the end result was that by the end of the month he was back to work full time and didn't take any more sick time for the duration of his employment with the company.

If you get a sick note in with 'stress' or similar, contact the employee in the first or second week of absence. Have a face-to-face welfare meeting and find out what's causing him difficulties and see if you can do anything to support him. The sooner you start to address issues, the sooner they're likely to be resolved and the employee can come back to work.

Where the employee seems to be suffering a fairly low level type of stress condition try to agree a gradual return to the workplace. You may need to involve his GP or your OMA. The approach will vary depending on individual circumstances, but in many cases you will find that by bringing the employee in to work for a few hours a week to start with, then increasing by half a day or a day each week, you will have the employee back at work within a four-six week period.

Case study

'Return to Work' is a programme run by employee assistance provider ICAS. It originated in Australia, where the company achieved an 86 per cent success rate in getting employees with depression back into work within an average of four weeks.

Getting back to work is not only important from a personal financial point of view, but can also play a fundamental part in recovering from depression.

Joe had been feeling the stress mounting for many months at his work for a bank. His team had been cut and he was doing three people's jobs.

"That kind of pressure is fine for a couple of months, but you can't sustain it in the long term. I didn't realise how bad things were until I crashed my car. All of a sudden my world just caved in," Joe said.

The crash acted as a trigger to a breakdown and depression followed. Joe was signed off work and for the first few weeks all he could was to sit at home and do nothing. Fortunately, his company used the ICAS 'Return to Work' programme and were able to offer him a route back into work.

ICAS contacted Joe at home and suggested that he start by seeing a psychologist on a regular basis. After a few weeks the ICAS consultant began to work out a step-by-step programme for Joe to return to work, which involved working closely with him and his line manager. Joe was keen to get back to work, but the issues that had triggered his depression in the first place needed to be addressed.

"My line manager has been first class," he said. "She recognised that I couldn't keep up the volume of work I had before and has taken steps to sort out the lack of support."

Joe started by visiting the office for a few weeks before starting work. His consumer-facing work began again on a phased basis gradually increasing and he is now back again full time.

Introduction To SSP

Statutory Sick Pay (SSP) is the minimum level of payment an employer pays to the majority of employees who are off work sick. It is paid to employees who are unable to work because of sickness. It is paid by the employer for up to a maximum of 28 weeks and in the same way and at the same time as an employee's normal wages. If SSP ends, an employee can claim Incapacity Benefit.

SSP is not paid for specific illness or treatment, but to all employees who are incapable for work and who satisfy the conditions for payment.

An employee must have worked for you under a contract of service.

It is useful to know the jargon connected with SSP.

Lower Earnings Limit (LEL). This is the minimum level of earnings that an employee's average weekly earnings must reach, in a specific period, for them to get SSP.

National Insurance contributions (NICs). Employees who pay Class 1 NICs can, or could if their earnings were high enough, be entitled to SSP.

Percentage Threshold Scheme (PTS). Under this scheme an employer may be able to recover some, or all, of the SSP he has paid to his employees in a tax month.

Period of Incapacity for Work (PIW). This is a period of sickness lasting at least four or more days in a row. All days of sickness count towards the total number of days, even non-working days. If there are fewer than four consecutive days, there is no PIW and you need take no action.

Qualifying Days (QDs). SSP is a daily payment and is usually paid for the days that the employee would normally work QDs. SSP is not paid for the first three QDs in any period of sickness, unless it falls within a linking period. You can decide not to use the contracted working days if, for example, your workforce operates a varied work pattern each week. For simplicity, you may want to have the same days each week as the QDs, but you must first reach agreement with your workforce or their representative(s) about which days will be QDs. There must be at least one QD in each week running from Sunday to Saturday. Bank holidays and other non-working days do not alter the normal pattern of QDs. Employers are liable to pay this to all their employees who satisfy all the qualifying conditions when they are off work sick.

Waiting Days (WDs). SSP is not payable for the first three QDs in a PIW. These are called WDs. They are not always the first three days of sickness, as the employee may have been sick on non-QDs.

Where PIWs are linked and all three WDs have been served in the first PIW, there will be no WDs in any later linked spells of sickness. But, if all three WDs have not been served in the first PIW, any remaining WDs must be served at the beginning of the next linked PIW or series of linked PIWs.

Week. For working out SSP entitlement and payment, a week is a period of seven days, starting on Sunday and ending on Saturday.

To receive SSP an employee must be:

- sick for at least four or more days in a row (including weekends and bank holidays); This is known as a Period of Incapacity for Work; and

- earning, before tax and National Insurance, an amount equalling or exceeding the LEL.

From 1 October 2006, any qualifying employee receives SSP. The Age Discrimination legislation has removed the requirement that an employee be aged between 16 or over and under 65. Earnings are averaged over an eight-week period before the employee's sickness began. This period may vary slightly, depending on whether he is paid weekly or monthly, or at other intervals. If he has just started his job, the calculation may be different.

To get SSP, the employee must only notify you that he is sick. If you only pay SSP, you cannot insist that he tells you:

- in person; or

- earlier than the first qualifying day or by a set time; or

- on a special form; or

- on a medical certificate; or

- more than once a week during his sickness.

You can, however, put in specific notification conditions where you pay OSP. It's for this reason that I generally recommend that an employer offers some OSP.

When the employee has been sick for eight consecutive days, you may ask for evidence that he is sick. This will usually be in the form of a sick note from his doctor.

Where notification of illness is late, you can withhold payment of SSP for the period of the delay if the notification was given outside these time limits and you do not accept there was good cause for delay. If you decide to withhold payment, you should treat the date of the late notification as the first day of sick absence.

He must be off work sick for four or more days in a row to be able to get SSP from you. However, if your employee has been sick for four or more days in a row and sick absence continues, but he is not entitled to SSP, you must complete form SSP1, or your own computerised version, so that he can claim Incapacity Benefit from the Jobcentre Plus or social security office.

Where a Period of Incapacity for Work (PIW) is separated from an earlier PIW by eight weeks (that is 56 days) or less, the two absences 'link' and are treated as one PIW.

A PIW must always be formed before there can be a link; in other words, your employee must be sick for at least four or more days in a row.

Odd days of sickness do not form a PIW and cannot link.

If any of the exclusions listed below apply to your employee, he is not entitled to SSP and must be given form SSP1.

- He was not sick for four, or more, days in a row.

- He always earned less than the lower earnings limit a week.

- She is within the 18/26 week exclusion period due to pregnancy or recently having had a baby.

- He has already had 28 weeks worth of SSP from you and this new spell of sickness links to the last one.

- He was not entitled to SSP the last time they were sick, for any reason, and this spell of sickness links to that one.

- He was getting Incapacity Benefit from DWP within the last eight weeks.

- He started or returned to work for you after getting Incapacity Benefit from DWP and is a Welfare to Work beneficiary who is sick within the first 104 weeks of starting or returning to work for you.

If the employee's weekly average earnings before deductions such as tax and National Insurance reach the LEL or above, he will be eligible to receive SSP.

If an employee is receiving SSP for a pregnancy-related illness at the start of or in the four weeks before her baby is due, SSP will stop and any entitlement to

Statutory Maternity Pay (SMP) or Maternity Allowance (MA) will start automatically.

If she is entitled to SMP or MA, she will not receive SSP for 26 weeks, starting with the day of entitlement to those payments.

If she is not entitled to SMP or MA, she will not receive SSP for 18 weeks, starting with either the Sunday of the week her baby is born or the Sunday of the week she is absent from work for a pregnancy-related illness.

Appendices

Appendix 1

Health screening form

Name

Please answer the following questions and give details if any of the answers are 'Yes'.

Do you, or have you ever suffered from the following?

Question	Yes/No	Details
Eye trouble, injury or defect not corrected by spectacles?		
Hearing difficulties?		
Is your sense of smell intact?		
Do you suffer from asthma or breathlessness?		
Back trouble, back ache or back injury?		
Difficulty in moving, sitting, bending or lifting?		
Do you have difficulty lifting or moving weights of up to xx lbs?		

Weakness of hand, wrist, arm or leg?		
Hernia or rupture?		
Epilepsy, blackouts or fainting?		
Do you suffer from claustrophobia or have difficulty in working at heights?		
Do you suffer, or have you ever suffered from, any clinical psychiatric conditions?		
Do you suffer from any medical conditions or injuries past or present which may affect your work?		
Have you had any days off due to sickness in the last 12 months? If the answer is 'yes' please indicate how many and the duration of each absence.		
Are you currently taking prescribed medicine?		

Are you currently under the care of a doctor or other medical professional?		
Has your employment ever been terminated on grounds of ill health or poor attendance?		

Declaration of Health

I confirm that the above information is true to the best of my knowledge. I understand and acknowledge that should I make a false statement regarding my medical history any offer of employment will be withdrawn.

Data Protection

I give permission for my information to be collected and processed for the purposes of recruitment and selection under the Data Protection Act.

Signature ....

Name ....

Date ....

Appendix 2

Sample absence management procedure

1. Introduction

As an employer, the Company has an obvious wish to ensure regular attendance at work on the part of its employees. In addition, as a good employer, it wishes to take an interest in the health and welfare of the people whom it employs. It also seeks to ensure that undue pressure is minimised for those people whose attendance record is good and whose workload is increased as a result of staff sickness. This procedure is designed to provide a framework within which the Company can achieve these important objectives.

The procedure sets out some formal steps to provide such a framework, but this does not prevent managers from carrying out a supportive welfare role by informally meeting staff with health difficulties and assisting them in any way which may be appropriate.

Throughout this procedure, all information concerning an employee's health will be treated in the strictest confidence.

As part of a line manager's role, home visits to employees on long-term sickness absence, or in other circumstances where the line manager thinks it appropriate, are positively encouraged.

Regard must be had to the Disability Discrimination Act 1995 (DDA), which requires employers to provide reasonable assistance, resources and support to employees with a long-term physical or mental impairment, whether that came about before or since employment started. If the line manager does not know if the employee's condition would constitute a disability, then he should work on the basis that it is and make all such reasonable adjustment to enable the employee to return to work.

2. Short-term sickness

Short-term absences may be defined as those which last for less than eight calendar days (including weekends and bank holidays), and are therefore certified by the individual rather than by a medical practitioner. In considering employees' records of absence of this nature, line managers will take into account the pattern as well as the total amount of sickness absence.

First stage

If a line manager feels that there is an unusually high level of sickness absence, for instance more than ten days within a twelve-month period, then he should meet the employee in the context of an informal welfare discussion. The first assumption should be that the employee has been absent for genuine medical reasons, unless there is specific evidence to the contrary. This should be made clear to the employee, so that there are no grounds for believing that an attempt to discipline him concerning absences is being made at this stage. The employee should be encouraged to talk about his reasons for absence, what medical or other help is being provided to him at present and whether he would like the Company's assistance in any way to try to resolve the problems.

Second stage

Where short-term absences continue to take place, despite the above counselling and offers of assistance, the line manager should meet the employee again. As before, the interview should normally be held in the context of a counselling and welfare discussion, but on this occasion, the desirability of a referral for independent medical advice should be discussed. If both the Company and the employee agree that this would be helpful in identifying and remedying the problem, arrangements should be made by the line manager for this to happen, with any necessary fees paid for by the Company. Following the meeting, the line manager should write to the employee, confirming the main points covered, noting any assistance which has been offered and indicating that the employee's record will be kept under review.

Third stage

If there is still no improvement within the next two or three months (or if absences start to recur after that period) the line manager should see the employee again. At this stage, if it has not been done before, arrangements must be made for independent medical advice to be obtained, on the same terms as stage two. Where that advice does not identify an underlying medical condition and there are no other mitigating factors, a letter should be sent to the employee making it clear that his attendance record is not acceptable and that an immediate and sustained improvement must be made if future employment is not to be jeopardised.

It may be that the employee refuses to undergo a medical examination. He should be encouraged to attend, but if there is still a refusal the employee cannot be forced to comply. However, such a refusal does not prevent the employer making a decision as to appropriate actions. This would include a decision to dismiss. It is for the employer to make a reasonable judgement on all the facts which may be available, which should include medical evidence if possible. The decision may be made in the absence of medical evidence if the employee objects without reason.

Consideration of termination of employment

If after a further short period (the length of which will be determined by circumstances), there is still no improvement, termination of employment will be considered. At this stage it becomes important to decide whether the absence is genuinely for ill-health or if there is no underlying medical reasons for the employee's sickness absences.

If there is an underlying reason for the sickness absence, the context of termination is an inability of the employee to properly discharge his duties. In this case, consideration should be given to other employment options, such as redeployment to an easier job, reductions in hours or adaptations to the existing job role. If these would present an acceptable solution, they may replace a decision to terminate the employment. His director should discuss the problem frankly and fully with the employee and then notify him of the decision made in the light of that discussion. A right of appeal to the Chief Executive should be given.

If there is no underlying medical reason for the absences, the employee will be taken through the disciplinary procedure and may ultimately be dismissed for some other substantial reason (SOSR).

Deliberate non-attendance at work may be regarded as gross misconduct, depending on the circumstances and therefore the employee should be informed that the result of a disciplinary hearing may be dismissal without notice.

Companion

At all stages of the formal procedure, employees have the right to be accompanied by a trade union representative or work colleague. Companions are able to help the employee prepare for the meeting, help him put his case, make representations, ask questions on his behalf and also sum up the case for the employee. However, companions may not answer questions on behalf of the employee.

3. Long-term sickness

The circumstances which give rise to absence of this type are usually quite different to those causing short-term absence. These will almost always be cases where an employee has a substantial and often on-going illness, or has been subject to some form of major injury. Because absence is long-term, it will be supported by a doctor's or hospital medical certificate.

The approach set out above for dealing with short-term absences is unsuitable for these circumstances. Instead, decisions are required to be taken in the light of the medical evidence and on the basis of balancing the needs of the Company and the capabilities of the employee.

Any employee who has been absent on certified sick leave for more than a month should by then have had contact with his line manager by telephone and/or by visits to ascertain his progress and to determine whether there is any practical assistance which the Company could give. This should be done in the context of genuine welfare assistance and not in any way so as to intrude into the employee's privacy, or else harass the employee as to when he will be coming back.

Provided that the employee agrees to it, the line manager should ensure that there is continued contact with the employee. This ensures that the employee does not feel forgotten by the Company.

Return to work

When an employee who has been long-term sick returns to work, his line manager should arrange to see him at the earliest opportunity to provide a welcome, ensure that he is fit for work (some people come back too soon because they are concerned about their jobs or because they go through the time limits for reduction in pay), and to update him on the current work in the department. Any problems of a major nature, such as not being really fit for work, should be referred to a director.

Under the DDA, there must be an assessment of the support and needs required for the employee to attend work. This includes looking at issues such as reduced hours for a period of rehabilitation (or longer), reasonable adjustments to the workplace and/or working conditions, reasonable adaptations or modifications to the premises and equipment and possible reallocation of duties.

Reasonable time off to attend medical appointments must also be given.

Incomplete recovery

If the employee is unlikely to recover sufficiently to enable a return to his full previous duties, the possibilities of finding alternatives or a reduced level of work must be considered. There is no obligation to create an unnecessary job to meet the employee's needs, but all reasonable steps should be taken to identify a job which the employee is able to do – where appropriate with the benefit of training and again by making suitable adaptations to the workplace and/or equipment.

A further possibility, if the employee agrees, is practical assistance (time off, references and so on), in the finding of less onerous or more suitable employment outside the Company.

No prospect of recovery

In cases where it becomes clear from all the evidence, and after proper assessment under the DDA, that it is really not practicable for the employee to return either to his previous job or to other employment within the Company, termination on grounds of ill-health needs to be considered. This must be considered in consultation with the employee and it is not in any sense a disciplinary matter.

The ultimate decision should be taken by the employee's director and only after the receipt of medical reports which support the view that there will not be fitness for work in the foreseeable future and normally not until at least six months has occurred. In considering timescales, the nature of the position held by the employee, the importance of replacing him and the feasibility of providing interim cover are valid factors, so an early decision may in some cases be appropriate.

If termination is felt to be necessary, the employee must be seen by his director and advised beforehand that he has a right to be accompanied by a fellow employee or trade union representative. Sufficient time should be allowed for the employee to arrange for the companion and this may be of the order of ten days to two weeks. The employee should be informed of the medical conclusions, asked for his views, consulted regarding the feasibility of alternative employment and presented with the realities of the situation. It should also be ascertained that the employee is fully aware of any entitlement to state benefits.

There may be agreement that termination is the only option. But it may be necessary to terminate without the employee's agreement and if so the employee must be advised of a right of appeal to the Chief Executive in this case.

Terminal illness

In cases where it is clear that illness is leading to death in the near future, it would be inappropriate to embark on formal procedures and welfare assistance to the employee and his family should be provided as far as possible.

Appendix 3

3.1 Letter to an employee who is refusing to talk to you

Jane Jones

Address

Date

<u>By Hand</u>

Dear Jane

Welfare Meeting

Further to my letter dated 3 April 2008 in which I asked if you would attend an examination by our occupational health advisor, I note that we have not yet received a reply from you.

As you have now been absent from work for three months, I must advise you that as an organization we are under a duty to take medical advice and using that advice, do what we can to help you return to work.

In the last few months, I have made several attempts to meet with you so that we can fully understand the nature of your difficulties. To date you have indicated that you do not want to meet. We have respected your wishes and allowed you time to recover.

However, as things seem to be no better, the time has come when we are obliged to look at other options for helping you. You have made it clear that you don't want to talk to either your line manager or myself directly. Therefore, I have arranged for an external HR advisor, Kate Russell, to meet with you to have a chat about your condition and to ascertain what further we can do to help you. Kate will contact you directly to arrange a time and place to meet.

If you have any queries or concerns about any of the foregoing, or need us to make appropriate adjustments to allow you to attend, please let me know and I will do what I reasonably can to resolve them.

Yours sincerely

John Green

HR Manager

3.2 Follow up letter to an employee who is refusing to talk to you

Jane Jones

Address

Date

By Hand

Dear Jane

Thank you for sending me the form agreeing to see our Occupational Health Advisor. I have set the process in motion and you will be contact to arrange a meeting. Once that has happened, we will arrange our own welfare meeting.

I confess that I don't understand why you feel yourself unable to meet with us and why this has become such an issue. Nothing in the conversations so far has really explained it. Please accept my assurances that you have nothing to fear. We simply want to understand through an informal conversation with you how matters stand and to work with you to promote your recovery.

Carrying out a welfare meeting with an employee who has been unwell for some time is a standard procedure. In following this process you are in no way being treated differently from the way any other sick employee would be treated. However, it is a necessary part of the process that we meet.

I shall be in touch in the next week or so to set up a date for our meeting.

Kind regards

John Green

HR Manager

Sample letter to doctor and health questionnaire

Mr A Smith
Kings Hospital
Kings Beaching
Northants
NN8 1SD

21 July 2003

Dear Mr Smith

**Re: Joanne Brown, DOB 6.8.65, 4 The Terrace,
Kings Beeching, Northants, NN8 2RG**

Joanne Brown has been employed by Easi-Buy Ltd as an Administration Supervisor since August 2000. She supervises a small team who process orders placed by customers. They also prepare and send out invoices. Joanne is office-based most of the time, although she occasionally visits customers at their premises.

I understand that she has been referred to you for investigation and treatment of her symptoms which she has described to us as primarily severe abdominal pains. She has given us permission to write to you as she has been suffering significant periods of ill health (see enclosed statement of permission).

We are keen to do what we can to help her. In a recent discussion, we elicited that she feels more unwell in the early morning and have therefore agreed with her that she may start work an hour later.

Joanne has told us that she has been undergoing a series of tests for food intolerance and a range of other conditions, including Crohn's Disease and irritable bowel syndrome. She has also been considering asking to be put on an elimination diet.

We would like to find out more about her condition, so that we can decide what we can do to help and what is the best course of action.

Attached is a questionnaire and an addressed pre-paid envelope. I would be grateful if you could complete this as fully as possible. Please contact me on 01844 511511 if you have any queries. You should send your invoice marked for my attention.

Thank you very much for your assistance in this matter. I look forward to hearing from you.

Yours sincerely

Mrs Gillian Joyce

Finance Director

Medical questionnaire

NAME: Joanne Brown

Please give your opinion regarding the general state of Joanne's health.

Please specify the medical condition from which she is suffering.

Please advise on the timescale for her recovery.

What has Joanne been tested for?

What were the test outcomes?

What treatment has she received?

Is she receiving treatment now? If so, please specify what.

Will she be able to continue to work in her present job role, either full time or part time?

If Joanne is unable to continue in her present job role, what type of duties might she be able to undertake?

What special needs might arise?

What in your view can we do to help her?

Any other general comments?

Name:

Signature:

Date:

Appendix 5

Some key points from the Court of Appeal in Hatton and others in 2002

An employer is usually entitled to assume that the employee can withstand the normal pressures of the job, unless he knows of some particular problem or vulnerability.

The employer is generally entitled to take what he is told by his employee at face value, unless he has good reason to think to the contrary. Factors that are likely to be relevant in considering whether or not the employer is liable include the nature and extent of the work done by the employee and signs from the employee of impending harm to health.

To trigger a duty to take steps, the indications of impending harm to health must be plain enough for any reasonable employer to realise that he should do something about it. The employer is only in breach of the duty of care if he fails to take reasonable steps, bearing in mind the magnitude of the risk, the gravity of any harm, the costs and practicability of preventing it and the justifications for running the risk.

The size and scope of the employer's operation are relevant in deciding what is reasonable.

An employer who offers a confidential advice service, with referral to appropriate counselling or treatment services, is unlikely to be found to be in breach of duty.

If the only reasonable step to alleviate the stress is to dismiss or demote the employee, then the employer will not be in breach of duty in allowing a willing employee to continue in the job. In all cases, it is necessary to identify the steps which the employer both could and should have taken before finding him in breach of his duty of care. Where the harm suffered has more than one cause, the employer should only pay that proportion of the harm suffered which is attributable to his wrongdoing.

Useful Contacts

ACAS	www.acas.org.uk
Data Protection	www.informationcommissioner.gov.uk
DWP	www.dwp.gov.uk
EHRC	www.equalityhumanrights.com
EFT	www.emofree.com
HMRC	www.hmrc.gov.uk
HSE	www.hse.gov.uk
National Statistics	www.ons.gov.uk
NLP	www.nlpconnections.com
People Alchemy	www.peoplealchemy.co.uk
Work Foundation	www.theworkfoundation.com
Yoga	www.yoga.co.uk

Author

Contact the author directly.

Email	Kate@russell-personnel.com
Website	www.russell-personnel.com

Off the Sick List! Training

To gain some extra practical experience, we have designed a workshop to give delegates the opportunity to really hone their experience.

Off the Sick List! is a one day workshop, designed to provide delegates with a practical skills in carrying out effective sickness management techniques. Making extensive use of practical exercises, including dealing with difficult questions and recording the delegates as they carry out role play, this workshop will help delegates grasp the practical requirements of sickness absence interviewing.

Because there is so much practical work, delegate numbers are limited to six a day

Course outline

- The law relating to sickness absence

- The process of managing sickness absence

- Question technique - purpose of questions, types of questions, the question funnel

- Structuring the meeting for effective outcomes

- Building rapport

- Listening skills

- Note taking

To find out more or to make a booking call
0845 644 8955.

148

Employment Law Training

Other practical workshops delivered by Russell Personnel & Training are set out below.

- Don't recruit a problem! Getting recruitment right

- Introduction to discipline, grievance and dismissal

- Contracts of employment

- Managing redundancy

- Redundancy representatives training

- Introduction to appraisal

The contents and duration of the workshops vary. You can get a flavour of what's covered by visiting our website **www.russell-personnel.com**

We will be happy to tailor a workshop to your specific requirements.

To find out more or to make a booking call
0845 644 8955.

Law on the Move

Staying up-to-date with employment law is time consuming (and can be a bit dull), but *Law on the Move* changes all that and makes employment law updates quick, easy and interesting.

Law on the Move is an audio employment update, ideal for listening to in the car. If you listen to the CD on your way to work for ten minutes a day over the course of a week once every three months the job's done; you're up-to-date with no pain. MP3 downloads are also available.

Praise for *Law on the Move*

This is an excellent resource. In a fast changing environment, with often little time to truly consider the implications of change, the ability to listen while travelling is a great idea. I have used this while in the car and on the train and found it extremely helpful. *Adrian Christy, CEO, Badminton England*

It's a brilliant idea! Really easy to listen to. Ian *Whitley, Manager, Programme Delivery, Honda Institute*

Law on the Move gives a helping hand in keeping up-to-date with employment law. Russell Personnel & Training are also delighted to support Dogs for the Disabled (www.dogsforthedisabled.org**). 10% of the subscription fee is given to support their activities.

To find out more (and put the enjoyment back into employment) call **0845 644 8955.**